Ten-Fold Marketing

Growing Your Business by Growing Your Heart

By Marianne Carlson

Ten-Fold Marketing: Growing Your Business by Growing Your Heart
by Marianne Carlson
Published by
Emcie Media LLC
2607 S. Woodland Blvd. #198
DeLand, FL 32720
www.emcie.com

Published by Emcie Media LLC, DeLand, Florida

Trademarks: Emcie Media, the Emcie Media logo, Ten-Fold, Ten-Fold Marketing, Ten-Fold Foundation, the Ten-Fold logo, Growing Your Business by Growing Your Heart, the heart/graph logo, Live Ten-Fold, livetenfold.com, emcie.com, and related trade dress are trademarks or registered trademarks of Emcie Media LLC, and cannot be used without permission.

Cover and interior design and layout by Emcie Media
Back cover photo by Exulting Images, Longwood, Florida

ISBN-13: 978-0615671178

ISBN-10: 0615671179

Dedication

This work is dedicated to the men and women of the U.S. Army who helped me realize that Duty, Honor and Country are not just words, and for whom Selfless Service is a daily commitment.

Table of Contents

"What I know
for sure
is that
what you give
comes back
to you."

- Oprah Winfrey

Foreword

When women ask me the secret to my success, I often tell them I do well by doing good. By taking the time to help others, through little acts of kindness -- by caring – I believe good things have come to me personally and financially.

But ever since 1999, when I founded Women For Hire as the first and only company providing recruitment services for talented, career-driven professional women, job seekers who email me at all hours of the day and night have been amazed when I reply personally with advice. At my Spark & Hustle conferences for current and aspiring women entrepreneurs, small business owners love that I mingle with them for hours – instead of only preaching to them from the stage. In the weeks and months afterwards, they, too, are stunned when I personally reply to their emails or pick up the phone and call.

At ABC's *Good Morning America*, where I do a weekly exclusive deals segment featuring great products, viewers who complain about vendors are blown away when they get an email or call from me, the woman they see on TV, offering to help.

In the days following Hurricane Katrina, I flew to Houston – determined to *do something* to help people displaced by the storm. The story of how I helped one young woman get back on her feet ended up in newspapers and TV.

Why do I do this?

For starters, I believe it's *the right thing to do*. Not just to experience the feel-good sensation in your heart. But it's also strategic: I know that by creating good will, viewers and attendees at my events appreciate me more. In the future, when they're trying to decide whether to buy my services, they're much more likely to do so if I have reached out to help them. This strategy is hardly mine alone: old school politicians once routinely handed out Thanksgiving turkeys to poorer constituents – knowing that their largesse would rebound come Election Day.

My friend Marianne Carlson, dubbed "The Granny Geek" at Spark & Hustle, knows what I'm talking about. She's as passionate as the most selfless grandma about helping others succeed in marketing, with the energy of a teenager to help others grow their bottom line.

Marianne truly believes that the sacrifices we make for others benefit us in real, measurable and significant ways – and that we can use that truth to market and grow our businesses. On these pages, you'll be inspired by the countless examples of using your time and talent in unexpected ways -- and you'll be armed with ideas to make it happen for yourself and your business.

Tory Johnson, Founder & President
Women For Hire and **Spark & Hustle**
Workplace Contributor,
ABC's *Good Morning America*

"Your guidepost
stands out
like a ten-fold
beacon in the night:
Duty,
honor,
country."

General Douglas MacArthur
to the cadets of the
U.S. Military Academy

Acknowledgements

I would like to begin by formally thanking the men and women of the United States Armed Forces, and especially those members of the US Army with whom I've had the honor to work both in Iraq and at West Point. While I believe that every American owes them a debt of gratitude, the debt I owe them is far deeper and more personal. It is the Army's core value of "Selfless Service" that is at the core of the concepts that support this book and the Ten-Fold Marketing philosophy, and the skills and life lessons I have learned from my time with the Army have literally changed my life.

The inspiration for this book came to me first from my good friend, Kat Feder, in a speech she had given at one of our networking events. As she finished her remarks, she closed with these words about giving back to the community. "I truly believe," she said, "that whenever you do something good for someone else, it comes back to you tenfold." Although I had heard that sentiment before, something about Kat's presentation had started me thinking about it as a marketing strategy, and eventually as a topic for a book. Her talk got me to thinking about the many famous people who are well known for their philanthropy, and it seemed to me that the more they gave away, the richer they became. And thus the book idea was born. So thank you, Kat. You were so right.

I have so many people to thank for their input and insight, without whom this book surely never would have come to be. A very special thank you to Tory Johnson for her beautiful forward, and for her immeasurable impact on the project both directly and indirectly. She is the absolute embodiment of the Ten-Fold philosophy, and her generosity, encouragement and support have been invaluable throughout the process.

To the many people who responded to my emails with stories and encouragement, thank you! There were far too many to list by name, but I am grateful to each of them. Most of the stories I received didn't make it into the book, but all of them gave me encouragement. Each of them was further proof of the theory behind Ten-Fold Marketing. And each of them provided me with examples of businesses large and small that are engaged in doing good in the world because it's the right thing to do. Their stories have lifted my heart and I hope they will lift yours as well. There really are good people in this world, and I have had the honor and sheer joy of getting to know many of them.

Thank you, specifically, to the many people who wrote to me, and who put me in touch with the CEOs whose stories are included here. They were instrumental in running interference for me so I could gain access to the inspiring CEOs for whom they work. My sincere gratitude goes out to Melina Metzger at Safetouch AutoGlass®, Linda Muskin at Braintree, Eva Lipson at Squeeze In, Danielle Killian at FormLA Landscaping, Judy Sultan at Xtreme Lashes, and Lauren Russ, Jennifer Kelly, and Jessica Aptman at ZocDoc. And of course, I want to thank the CEOs themselves, whose stories play such a vital role in the book. Their stories of philanthropy and caring have been inspiring to me, and I have personally been the recipient of their generosity in terms of both time and content.

And last, but certainly not least, I want to thank my husband, Don, who is my strength and constant support, and my daughters, Gretchen and Paula, who have provided encouragement and advice throughout the process. Thank you all so very much!

A Word about the framed quotes

Being a fan of pithy sayings and quotes, I've included a number of "framed" quotes like the one on the next page. In Part 5, I list the names of each of the quoted authors, along with a few words of description. I encourage you to read more about these brilliant thinkers, as there's much more to be learned from their wisdom.

"In this world,
it is not
what we take up,
but what we
give up
that makes us rich."

-Henry Ward Beecher

Preface

In 2010, I was encouraged by a trusted advisor to attend a conference that Tory Johnson had developed for female entrepreneurs. The conference called "Spark & Hustle" was touring around the country to rave reviews, and was gaining a remarkably enthusiastic fan base. When Spark & Hustle came to Orlando, I took my friend's advice and registered to attend. That conference was a real game-changer for me and for my business. Thank you, Jennifer Lee, for advising me to attend; thank you, Tory Johnson, for presenting such a powerful conference; and thank you to each of the speakers and attendees who helped make my experience that week all that it turned out to be.

I wrote this book for the Spark & Hustle community and for the many entrepreneurs who continue to inspire me with their passion, ingenuity and amazing heart. This book is for you, my BBFs – my Best Business Friends.

Some of you know my story, but for those who don't, I want to start with some background, because knowing where I come from will help you understand the thinking and the motives behind the concepts presented in the following pages.

My husband, Don, worked as a civilian employee of the US Defense Department, and we've spent most of our lives moving. From Indiana to Ohio, to Italy, to Belgium, to Vermont, to Germany, to New York, and finally to Florida. It's been a fascinating and exciting life, but every time we moved, I was back to looking for a job, and whenever we moved overseas, I was looking for a job on an American military base.

In the mid-nineties, while we were living in Belgium, I couldn't find work on the small American base near us, so I went back to school to complete my degree. The University of Maryland has an arrangement with the US Military, and there are small U of M education centers all over the globe, offering members of the military the opportunity to continue their education, no matter where they might be serving. At that time, there were no online courses, so my options were limited, and I ended up with a Bachelor's Degree in a subject I had absolutely no interest in whatsoever. Computers.

I eventually put that degree to work in Vermont, where I worked for the state's Judiciary as their Computer Support and Training Coordinator, a job I dearly loved. I could have died happy in Vermont. A big fish in a small pond, I knew every Judge and every Supreme Court Justice by name, and they knew me. I had a team of 18 Power Users, hand-picked and trained by me, who were the greatest team members any leader could ever hope for. And my job was more about communication, coaching and training than it was about computers, so I loved it. It broke my heart to leave Vermont, but duty called, and Don's job moved us next to Germany.

In Germany, I had a really hard time finding work. You see, the Army has a policy whereby the spouses of military members get hiring preference, and my husband isn't in the military. He's a civilian. So I didn't get the benefits of the hiring preference policy. Now, don't get me wrong. I believe that the policy is just and correct, and I fully support its purpose. These military members put their lives on the line for our country, and we uproot their families and disrupt their spouses' careers, and we don't begin to pay them enough for what they do. So I believe the least we can do is to try to keep their spouses employed.

But the policy did make it essentially impossible for me to get a job overseas. According to the policy, if a military spouse met the basic minimum requirements for a position, they had to offer it to them, and my name was never sent up to the hiring authority. And in 2001, when we moved to Germany, many military members were women, so the spouses in question were young men, all of whom had basic computer skills, and all of whom really wanted those great IT jobs. So a full year passed and I was never called for an interview.

It didn't matter that I had this wonderful academic and professional resume. It didn't matter that I had references from the Supreme Court of Vermont, or that I had graduated *Summa cum*

Laude from college. Once there was a military spouse who met the minimums, my application was essentially nullified. It happened time after time, and I began to worry about becoming obsolete. In an industry that changes every day, a year is a very long time. My skills were becoming obsolete and my degree was already passé. Microsoft had introduced a new operating system that I had never used, and everything I knew about computers would soon be useless or forgotten. I needed a job, and I needed it soon.

Then, at last, the Army called at the end of 2002, and offered me an interview. Relieved, excited, and more nervous than I'd ever been for a job interview, I met with the hiring officer for the G-6 Section of the 3rd Corps Support Command, 3d COSCOM, for short. He clearly didn't think I was the man for the job, but he offered me the position, expecting, I believe, that I would turn it down. You see, the only reason they hadn't given the job to a military spouse was because the job was deployable – meaning that whoever they hired could be deployed to any hotspot across the globe – and the military spouses didn't want a job with those strings attached!

But I had three compelling reasons for accepting the job:
1. I needed the job to rescue my career in IT. I was in no position to turn down the first job offer I'd had in over a year.
2. I didn't honestly think a deployment was likely. I mean, if you saw me, 45 years old, overweight, out of shape, and

completely devoid of any survival skills, you wouldn't think so either. The fact is, that I simply couldn't imagine a scenario in which the United States Army would want to send me into a war zone. It was never gonna happen.

3. This was not long after September 11th had rocked my world and changed my perspective on a lot of things. I said then, and I still say, that if my country really needed me, I'd go.

So I signed on the dotted line, and six months later, shipped off to Iraq for six months in hell that would change my life forever.

My time in Iraq was horrible, frightening, depressing, humiliating, disgusting, physically grueling, and emotionally draining. But it was also the most amazing experience of my life. It was my first time away from home, on my own, so it had that coming-of-age element to it, even though I was already a middle-aged mother of three. It was also a time of self-discovery and introspection that taught me two very important lessons about myself.

The first lesson was that life is short, and I'm too damn old to be doing something I hate for a living. I now realize that every person is born too old to do something they hate for a living, but it took me that road trip to hell to learn it for myself. I hated IT, and fixing computers, and running servers, and installing networks. I hated it. And I needed to find a different path.

The second important lesson I learned in the desert is that I am in love – 100%, to my core, in love – with the United States

Military. For six months, I had worked with people for whom Duty, Honor and Country are not just words, and it was a genuine privilege to serve with them. I needed out of IT, but if I could follow a different path, and remain in touch with the US Military, I believed I could be very happy indeed.

And so, when Don's job moved us next to New York state, I went looking for work at the US Military Academy at West Point. I applied for every job they had that I was even remotely qualified for. Every job, that is, except IT. And eventually, I was hired as a sort of "Project Coordinator" on a special project for the Chief of Staff of the Army. It was on that project that I learned my first skills as a web designer, and discovered the joy of doing what I really love for a living.

In 2005, I lost my son to suicide. I tell you that, not to gain your sympathy, but to offer you hope. Surely there is no greater pain than that one, and no greater obstacle to overcome. Yet I am here today, living proof that *There is life after whatever is hurting you today.* Time really does heal all wounds – even that one. And if you surround yourself with people who care about you, you can overcome anything. You can live again, laugh again, and even thrive.

After that tragedy, I became even more aware that when you help other people, you help yourself. That's the Army's core value that they call "Selfless Service", that has inspired me and encouraged me. And that's the undeniable truth that is the basis for this book.

When you perform selfless service, good things happen. They happen to the people you help, and they happen to the world at large. And, as you'll see as you read this book, they can happen to you and to your business.

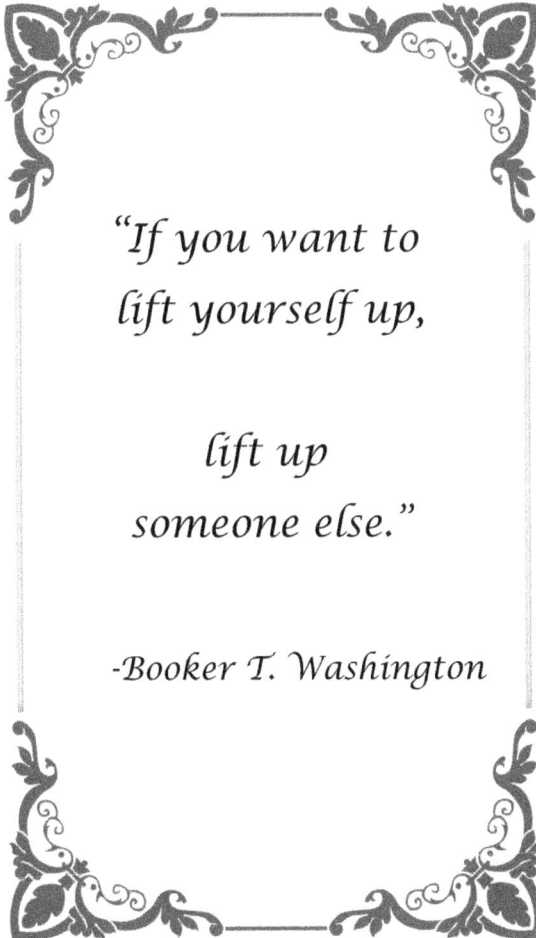

> "If you want to
> lift yourself up,
>
> lift up
> someone else."
>
> -Booker T. Washington

Part One

Introduction

*You can have
everything in life
that you want,*

*if you will just help
enough other people
get what they want.*

-Zig Ziglar

CHAPTER 1

What is Ten-Fold Marketing?

(And what is it not?)

I n 2009, Jason Kitterell[1] won over 19 thousand dollars in the California lottery. "I remember the day I bought the winning ticket," he later recalled. "I left work late that day and was debating whether to stop and buy my tickets at all. I always buy them on Thursdays. My son stays after school on Thursdays to work with a tutor, so I don't have to rush home. But that Thursday I was running later than usual.

"I passed a car that was broken down and the driver was a young woman. She was standing off in the grass with her little boy. I figure it was too hot to wait in the car and not safe anyway, so close to the highway. I felt bad for her and especially for the

---

[1] This story is based on one I heard a few years ago. The details (names, dates, etc.) are fictitious, but the story illustrates the concepts as well as any I've heard.

kid. And I worried that they might be stranded, so I pulled over. I parked on the shoulder in front of her car, and walked toward the two of them. As I approached, she picked up her son and I could see she was thinking I might mean her harm.

"So I stopped a few yards from her and shouted over the traffic noise, 'Do you need some help? Is someone coming for you?'

"She showed me her cell phone and told me her husband was on his way. 'OK, good,' I said to her, 'I think I'll wait here with you till he gets here. It's not safe for you here by yourself.' She said she didn't need me to do that, but I just didn't feel right leaving her there at the side of the road with a little kid. So I just stood there, and waited with her.

"After a while, I asked her name and the boy's name. I don't even remember their names now, but it kind of broke the ice and we talked a while about the weather and stuff. It was just a few minutes before her husband arrived. I could tell she knew him because she started walking toward the car before it was even stopped. As she walked toward his car, she thanked me for stopping and for keeping her company. Once I knew they were in good hands, I headed for home. I was feeling good – like I'd done a good deed. And I stopped on my way, and bought that winning lottery ticket.

"I can't tell you how many times since then I have thought about that woman and that little boy. If they hadn't broken down, I never would have stopped, and I would have arrived at the store a few minutes earlier. Or maybe I wouldn't have stopped at all. In either case, it seems pretty likely that somebody else would have bought that ticket and won the money. They say when you do something good, it comes back to you tenfold. I guess it's really true."

Jason Kitterell's story isn't all that unusual. In fact, if you think about it, I'm sure you can recall times in your own life when you were in the right place at the right time, because something happened to change your routine. Just like Jason, you may have benefited from circumstances that came about because of a choice you made to help another person. And that is a simple example of the theory we're going to explore over the course of this book.

But stories like Jason's are too simple and too rare to form the basis for your strategic marketing plan. You can't expect to turn a single good deed into a corporate success story. But I believe the concept behind it is so powerful and far-reaching, it can and does create success and prosperity in the lives and businesses where the theory is fully embraced. I believe that when companies and business leaders do good, they are at least ten times more likely to prosper than their counterparts who don't. And over the pages of this book, I will give you the evidence, the strategies, and the motivation to grow your own business by growing your heart.

Ten-Fold[2] Marketing, like any traditional marketing, is a strategy for creating a brand, or a product, or a service that people

---

[2] Ten-Fold is a trademark, pending registration, and is used throughout the book to identify a specific, branded marketing strategy. It's not a misspelling of the English word, *tenfold*.

will want to buy. But this strategy is anchored by a concentrated effort to do good in the world. This book will provide you with the understanding and the insights you'll need to create your own Ten-Fold Marketing strategy and lead your business – and your life - down a very rewarding path toward success and prosperity.

Robb Willer is a sociologist at the University of California at Berkeley, who has done research into the ways individuals overcome selfishness to contribute to the social good. "It makes sense to be generous from a self-interested perspective," Willer says. "If you're generous, you receive more respect, you have more influence and people cooperate with you more." Willer's research demonstrates the science behind the strategy that this book is all about.

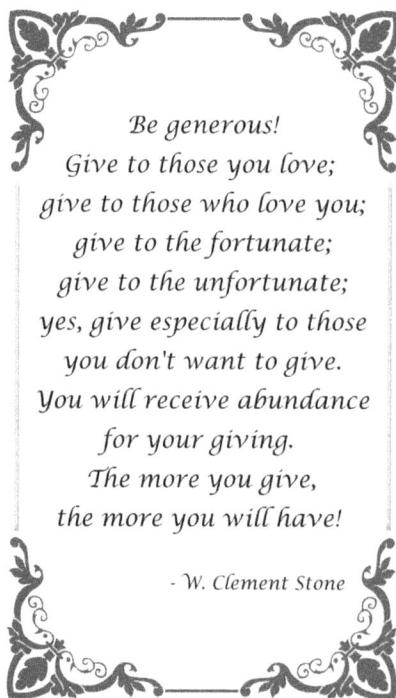

Be generous!
Give to those you love;
give to those who love you;
give to the fortunate;
give to the unfortunate;
yes, give especially to those
you don't want to give.
You will receive abundance
for your giving.
The more you give,
the more you will have!

- W. Clement Stone

What Ten-Fold Marketing is Not

Ten-Fold Marketing isn't new.

For decades – probably centuries – the world's greatest business leaders, and the people who advise them, have known that donating time, money, knowledge and passion for the greater good has been good for the bottom line. Consider the following excerpts from the writings of some of those leaders.

- Alex Shalman, the acclaimed personal development coach, lists on his website (www.alexshalman.com) his own Ten Daily Success Habits. Among them is the simple, but powerful commitment to "Help a person."

- Craig Harper (www.craigharper.com.au) also has a list of the Habits of Successful People. Among them he states, "They are generous and kind. They take pleasure in helping others achieve."

- In his book, *Beat the System*, Robert W. MacDonald lists 11 simple secrets of successful entrepreneurship. Secret # 8 is "Sharing wealth creates wealth."

- And a personal favorite of mine, the great Zig Ziglar has said this:

> *"You can have everything in life you want if you will just help enough other people get what they want."*

I could go on with this, but suffice it to say that it has long been recognized that successful people share a number of traits, characteristics and habits. And one of those is the "habit" of doing good for their fellow man.

Because selfless service is a common characteristic of our most successful entrepreneurs, I propose that by emulating those successful people and by practicing acts of selfless service, you can and will improve your own odds for success.

Ten-Fold Marketing isn't a Religious Dogma

You may be thinking that it's wrong or even immoral to think about doing good in the hopes of getting something in return, and I want to address that issue up front. It may well be true that God would prefer that you do your good deeds anonymously. I not qualified to speak to the values and teachings of any of the world's religions, and that is definitely not the purpose of this book.

Maybe the blessings from God require anonymous giving, and if that is your belief, I urge you to stay true to it.

But this book isn't about religious dogma, or about gaining God's favor. This book is about gaining your customers' favor, and building your business by sharing your assets with the people who need them. Your company's assets should be invested so as to bring about the greatest return, and I believe there's a place in every company's balance sheet for serving the community and the less fortunate among us. Doing good is good for your business. And it's definitely good for the people who are on the receiving end.

I believe that all of society benefits when business leaders engage in positive service to the community. If those businesses are financially stronger for having done so, that's an added benefit for them and for the community at large.

I don't believe for a moment that financial success is in opposition to the teachings of any of the world's major religions. But if you believe that remaining anonymous in your philanthropy is crucial to your spiritual health, by all means, remain anonymous. I would never suggest that anyone abandon their ethics or their faith in the pursuit of financial success.

It has been said that when you do something good for someone else, it will come back to you tenfold. In the following chapter, I present evidence that the concept of tenfold returns on voluntary giving is not new, nor is it a teaching limited to the Christian faith. The concept exists in the teachings of many religions and many cultures. In fact, it appears to be a global concept that is part of the human mentality, regardless of race, creed, status, or political bent. Ten-Fold Marketing is based on a universal human experience, which is one reason it can be so universally powerful.

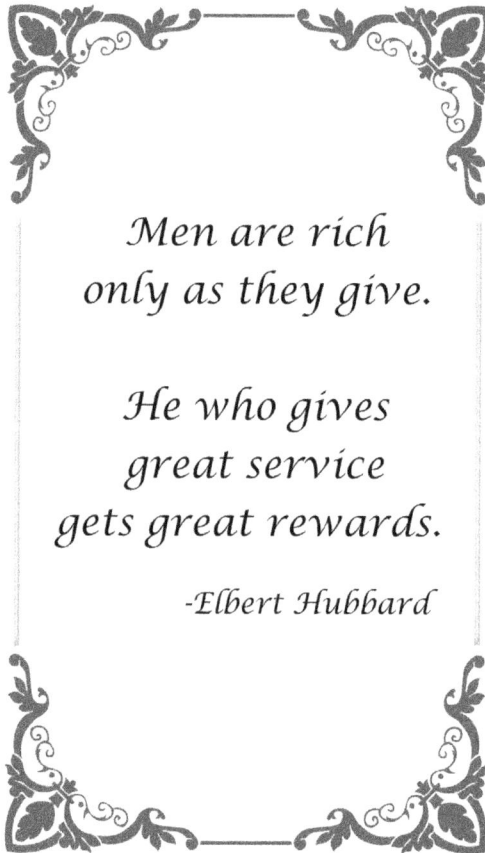

*Men are rich
only as they give.*

*He who gives
great service
gets great rewards.*

-Elbert Hubbard

One should
perform karma
with nonchalance

without expecting
the benefits

because
sooner or later
one shall definitely
get the fruits.

-Rig Veda

CHAPTER 2

Ten-Fold's Global Acceptance

W e've all heard it said that when you do something good for someone else, the good comes back to you tenfold. But where did that idea originate? And is it really true?

Certainly, the importance of the doing good toward one's fellow man is shown in the Old and New Testaments, but it has also been seen in other religious works through the ages. In the Koran, for example, the Holy Book of Islam, we find: "He that doeth good Shall have ten times As much to his credit" [Sura VI:160].

It's not apparent where or when the concept originated, but research shows evidence of it dating back long before the birth of Christ, and in cultures and societies all over the world. The Shramana of ancient India (dating back as far as 600 BC) espoused the concept, and spread it, along with many of their traditions and beliefs to the Buddhist and Hindu practitioners throughout the region.

The strength of the relationship between good deeds and personal reward is especially well represented by the Hindu goddess, Lakshmi, who is revered as the goddess of wealth and prosperity, but also as the goddess of generosity. It is said that Lakshmi brings good luck to those who follow her tenets. She is believed to protect her devotees from all kinds of misery and money-related sorrows. The embodiment of both characteristics – both prosperity and generosity – in a single entity speaks to the Hindu belief that the two are indeed related and connected.

The concept of Karma, even the modern version as most Americans understand it, in which a person is rewarded – or punished – according to the moral quality of his actions toward others, has its origins in these ancient Indian religions, dating back as far as 1000 years before Christ.

Stories that support and illustrate the Ten-Fold concept abound in literature, including both Greek and Roman mythology. One example is the Greek myth of Baucis and Philemon, in which a poor couple take two travelers into their home. They are unaware that the travelers are in fact the gods, Jupiter and Mercury, and that the gods are testing their generosity. Their selfless behavior saves them from the flood and secures their respect in the eyes of the gods.

Folklore, fairy tales, and legends, passed down from one generation to the next, that teach the Ten-Fold concept, are found in every part of the world. "Do what's right, and you'll be rewarded" is a universal lesson taught by parents and societies around the globe.

One example is a Korean folk tale about a brush salesman who comes across of group of children who are sitting in the shade of a large tree, studying. He finds one young boy studying out in the blazing sun. When he asks why the boy doesn't sit in the cool shade with his peers, the boy replies, "My family is poor, and my father works as a day laborer in order to pay my school fees. My books, brushes, and papers are all the result of my father's hard work and sweat. I feel guilty reading on the cool floor while my father is working in a field in the summer heat. That is why I am reading this book under the burning sun. " The brush salesman is touched by the boy's compassion and rewards him with a gift of his finest brushes.

The Chinese, too, have a long history of embracing the Ten-Fold concept. Confucianism holds a number of elements as core to the morality of the individual and the society, and among all of these elements, Ren (Humanity) and Yi (Righteousness) are fundamental. Morality is measured in large part by actions taken toward nature and toward other individuals. The concept of reaping reward for moral behavior exists throughout the history of Confucian thought and continues today in the modern culture throughout China and the Asian continent.

The full extent and history of the Ten-Fold philosophy is beyond the scope of this book, but it is apparent that the concept has existed for many millennia and across geographic, religious and cultural boundaries. It seems that as a species, humans have embraced the ideals of generosity, caring and selfless service. Perhaps these ideals are ingrained in our DNA as a mechanism for perpetuating the species. Certainly they are ingrained in our cultures.

As individuals, and as a society, we embrace these ideals and honor those who live by them. We admire and respect the generous and caring members of our community, and we applaud their selfless service. The goodwill that exists for those individuals – and those businesses – is difficult to measure but easy to recognize. And that goodwill is a big part of the Ten-Fold Marketing strategy I'm about to unfold.

Love and kindness
are never wasted.
They always make a difference.

They bless the one
who receives them,
and they bless you, the giver.

-Barbara De Angelis

Part Two

Ten-Fold Marketing is Systemic

We shall serve
for the joy
of serving.

Prosperity shall flow
to us and through us
in unending streams
of plenty.

-Charles Fillmore

CHAPTER 3

Marketing isn't Advertising

This book is about marketing, and marketing isn't the same as advertising. In fact, for the purposes of this book, and to ensure your complete understanding of the Ten-Fold Marketing Strategy, I want you to expand your definition of marketing (whatever that might be) to one that truly embraces the entire company, and not just the Sales and Marketing Department.

I like to think of marketing as a company's strategy for increasing sales and profits. Once you accept that definition, you'll realize it goes well beyond advertising and public relations. For the purposes of this book, I define "*Marketing*" as *a systemic approach to increasing sales and enhancing a company's brand.* Advertising is a single component of the overall marketing strategy, but it is not the only part. In fact, over the next few chapters, I will share with you significant evidence that, for many successful businesses, advertising should play a relatively small role in the marketing strategy. But let me begin by expounding on my definition of marketing so you'll understand exactly what I mean, and can begin to formulate your own ideas for using Ten-Fold Marketing in your own business.

Defining Marketing

I've already stated my simple definition for the word marketing as *a systemic approach to increasing sales and enhancing a company's brand.* That is, in a nutshell, what I mean by "marketing". But let's crack that nut and peel away the shell, so we can get to the nourishing meat inside. Let's dig beneath the surface, because it is there that we'll find the full meaning and the great power behind the Ten-Fold Marketing strategy.

A Systemic Approach

I call it a *systemic approach* because it really does involve every aspect of your business, every employee, and every decision you make. If the purpose of marketing is to increase sales, then we have to look at all the factors that feed into a customer's decision to purchase your product or service. Your advertising campaigns are a piece of that pie, but they aren't the whole pie, because your customers consider a multitude of factors – both consciously and subconsciously – before they make their buying decisions. And every member of your team, every piece of correspondence, and every decision you make has consequences that can influence that decision making process.

When you think about your marketing as your systemic approach to increasing sales and enhancing your company's brand, you begin to realize that everyone in your company is part of that marketing effort. If your business is manufacturing widgets, then certainly, the people on your assembly line are part of that effort. The integrity of their work, and the quality of the widgets they produce have a direct impact on the customer's decision to buy. Quality products are more attractive to prospective customers than shoddy products, so the people most responsible for the quality of your widgets are definitely part of the marketing effort.

The direct relationship between the quality of your products and your ability to sell those products is apparent, and that is why I chose that relationship to focus on first. If the goal of your marketing effort is to increase sales, it stands to reason that maintaining a high level of quality should be a key component in those efforts. So, as you begin to explore the Ten-Fold Marketing strategies that could be implemented in your business, you'll want to keep in mind that increasing your company's sales and enhancing your company's brand are not just the Marketing Department's responsibility; everyone in your company shares in the responsibility.

Another fairly obvious connection exists between your level of customer service and your customers' willingness to purchase your goods and services. When customers receive helpful, prompt, and friendly service from your company, they are much more likely to buy from you again. They are also much more likely to refer their friends to you. And when they don't get great service, they are far more likely to look to one of your competitors the next time they need what you are selling. For that reason, it becomes important, as you plan your Ten-Fold Marketing strategies, to consider all the people in your company who interact directly with your customers.

From the receptionist to the billing department, every person on your payroll needs to be considered part of the marketing strategy. Every one of them has a role to play in increasing sales. It's your job, as the leader of your organization, to help them recognize their role and help them excel at it. And by reading this book, you're taking the first steps toward making that happen.

When you are kind
to someone in trouble,
you hope they'll remember
and be kind to someone else.
And it'll become like a wildfire.

-Whoopi Goldberg

Increasing Sales and Enhancing Your Brand

Now that you're beginning to think of your marketing strategy as a *systemic approach,* let's consider the second half of our definition – *increasing sales and enhancing your brand.* This is important because all too often, a company's marketing strategy focuses solely on increasing sales, and fails to account for the broader – and equally important – role of enhancing your company's brand.

What Exactly is a Brand?

If you ask that question to fifty business experts, you'll probably get fifty different answers. Many people, when asked to consider a company's brand, think only of the company's logo. For example, if you ask people "What is McDonald's brand?", they'll likely respond "The Golden Arches". Certainly their logo, the big yellow 'M', is part of their brand. But for McDonald's, that logo is a really small part of the company's overall brand. Ronald McDonald is also part of their brand. Their latest tagline is also part of that brand, but that's all advertising, and a company's brand encompasses a lot more than advertising.

So let me tell you how I define Brand, for the purposes of our discussion, and throughout the pages of this book. I define a company's brand as its public image – the way it is perceived by the public, and by its customers and potential customers. It's the emotions that are evoked when their name is spoken, or their company comes to mind. In short, your brand is your corporate image, and every company – no matter how large or how small – should be focused with fierce determination, on enhancing that image and building that brand.

McDonald's has built a brand by offering food fast and inexpensive, and that concept is a big part of their brand. But they also build their brand – and enhance it greatly – by sponsoring the Ronald McDonald House, a hotel of sorts, that serves as a home away from home so families can stay close by their hospitalized child. The company has built hundreds of these facilities in over 50 countries, and thousands of sick kids are helped every day because their families are nearby in affordable housing.

By engaging in this philanthropy, McDonalds helps countless deserving families, and countless chronically and terminally ill children. And in so doing, they enhance their corporate image – their brand – in the eyes of their customers.

The McDonald's brand, like most companies' brands, is multi-faceted and ever-changing. It's a huge international corporation, and that's one facet of their brand. It's a supporter of sick kids, and Olympians, and a host of other deserving charities, and that's another facet of their brand. McDonald's is a place that helps teenagers learn about the world of work, and that's another facet of their brand. They now offer fruit in every happy meal, and that's yet another facet of their brand. They also sell some products that are very high in calories, fat, and sodium. And that's a facet of their brand as well.

McDonald's understands the value of a powerful, positive brand, which is one of the reasons they give so generously to so many great charities. They understand that supporting a deserving charity is good for their business. They understand the value of Ten-Fold Marketing.

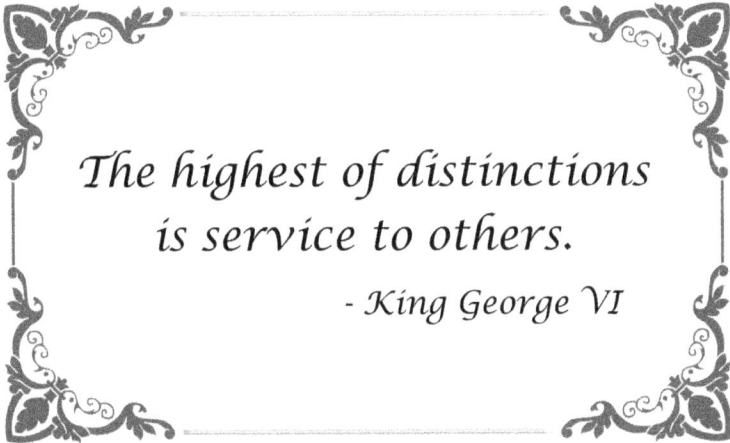

> *The highest of distinctions is service to others.*
> — *King George VI*

Why Your Brand is So Important

It's easy to recognize that branding is important to a big national company like Wal-Mart or Ford Motor Company. But why should your company care about building a strong brand? The answer lies in basic human psychology.

"People do business with people they know, like and trust." You've heard it said, and you've seen it in action. But the same is true for companies as well. People do business with *companies* they know, like and trust – and that's where you can reap the benefit from building a strong, positive brand, even if your company is just you!

Consider, as an example, the case of a small ice cream parlor in downtown Burlington, Vermont in 1978. The population of Burlington was at that time, about 20,000 people. (A mere shadow of the now booming metropolis of just over 40,000. Yeah, that's right. Forty thousand.) Ben Cohen and his best friend, Jerry Greenfield, had pooled their resources and renovated an old gas station near the city's center, and opened an ice cream parlor.

OK, so at this point I have to ask a question that is burning in my mind: How could two reasonable intelligent adults possibly believe that they could actually earn a living wage selling ice cream in a tiny town in northern Vermont? I mean, it's a little like selling snow to an Eskimo, isn't it? And yet, there they were, investing good money in building renovations and freezers! I mean, how many scoops of ice cream would you have to sell to recoup those costs, let alone earn a living wage for two adult men? And how many scoops of ice cream could they reasonably expect to sell in a tiny town in northern Vermont? It seems to me that these two men had developed a business model that couldn't possibly succeed. I can only marvel at their sense of entrepreneurial optimism.

Anyway, the shop opened its doors on May 5, 1978, with snow probably still covering the nearby lawns, and Ben & Jerry's Ice Cream Parlor was is business!

As crazy as it seems, and as unlikely, they were still in business a year later, and they decided to celebrate their first anniversary by giving away their product, hosting the first-ever "Free Cone Day". (Another hair-brained idea, it must have seemed to the causal observer.) They gave away ice cream cones to every man, woman and child that wandered into their store, and the news spread quickly throughout the community. This was a couple of decades before I moved to Vermont, so I was unaware of it at the time. But I can just imagine the chatter at the local diner. Vermonters are a very sensible lot, and this whole crazy notion must have seemed anything but sensible. And yet, somehow, the business thrived.

The goodwill gained in a small town by a gesture like that "Free Cone Day" is hard to measure, but impossible to deny, and it was a foreshadowing of far greater things to come. Today, Ben & Jerry's is a huge corporation with stores all over the country, and "Free Cone Day" has become an annual tradition. It has proven to be a real money-maker for them. It brings people into the shops – at the very start of their busy season – and reminds them of the Ben & Jerry's brand and their many awesome, delightful ice cream flavors.

Over a million free cones are given away each year, and charitable organizations are often present at the stores to enjoy a significant amount of fundraising success. Sometimes the event is scheduled to coincide with Earth Day, and it's not uncommon to find volunteers on hand with clipboards and voter registration forms to help those who would like to register to vote.

Perhaps Ben and Jerry were believers of the adage, "If a little bit is good, a whole lot is better", because it wasn't long before it was announced that they were giving away 10% of all their profits to charity. They started embracing – and actively supporting – many earth-friendly initiatives and causes that might have given their accountant cause for alarm. Their donations were substantial, but their profits were rising. They started packaging their ice cream in bio-degradable cartons, long before "bio-degradable" was a household word. And those cartons were a whole lot more expensive than the cartons used by their competitors. The phrase "Going Green" hadn't even been coined yet, so I think we can assume that their customers weren't exactly begging for earth-friendly packaging.   But they invested heavily in it, and turned it into a marketing strategy. And their business thrived and their profits kept climbing.

In 1992, Ben & Jerry's joined a campaign with the Children's Defense Fund, a national non-profit organization whose goal was to bring children's basic needs to the top of the national agenda. The CDF's website states that its mission is "to ensure every child a Healthy Start, a Head Start, a Fair Start, a Safe Start and a Moral Start in life and successful passage to adulthood with the help of caring families and communities."[3] It was a mission that both Ben Cohen and Jerry Greenfield were passionate about, so they committed themselves and their resources to it. They invested thousands, and their profits kept growing.

Eventually, the national media took notice, and the rest is history. In April 2000, Ben and Jerry sold the company to the

---

[3] http://www.childrensdefense.org

mega-grocer, Unilever, for $326 million. Somehow, two best friends from a tiny town in the frozen wilderness, had grown a brand – an ice cream brand, no less! – into an international phenomenon. And much of their success has been attributed to their corporate culture of charity, generosity and Ten-Fold Marketing.

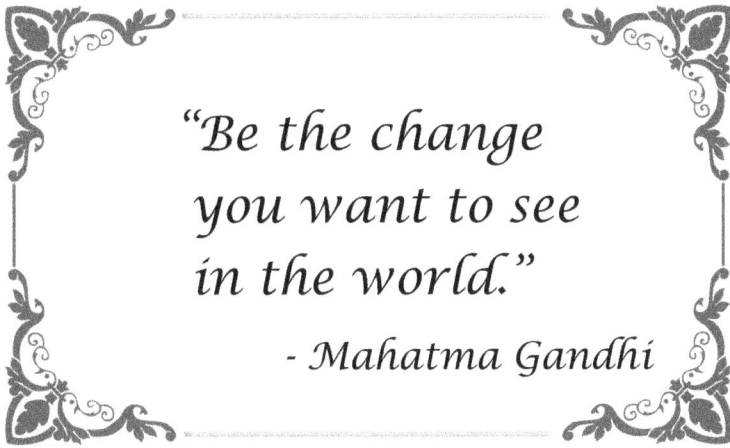

> "Be the change
> you want to see
> in the world."
> - Mahatma Gandhi

So consider the importance of your corporate brand and how you can grow it and capitalize upon its strength. Imagine how you can be the change you want to see in the world, and how that change can serve your community, your heart, your soul, and your company's marketing goals, all at the same time.

That is the message behind Ten-Fold Marketing, and its power is in its universal acceptance. We are a society - even a species – that values and rewards selflessness and generosity. When you give of yourself, your time, your money, and other resources, you reap the reward. Sometimes it's a direct reward, granted by the person or organization who directly benefited from your actions. Sometimes it's an indirect reward that surfaces out of a cloud of goodwill and common interests. And sometimes it's a personal reward, known only to you and your maker. But even the most personal rewards have outward benefits, and those can be the greatest rewards of all.

We've already talked about the Ten-Fold strategy as a systemic approach, and naturally any truly systemic approach has to start at the top. In the next chapter, I want to focus on how you can use the Ten-Fold concepts to enhance your leadership strategies, and help you be the change you want to see within your own organization.

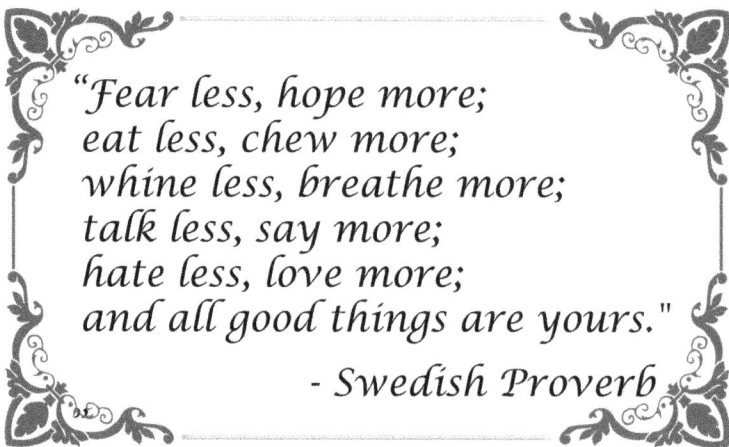

"Fear less, hope more;
eat less, chew more;
whine less, breathe more;
talk less, say more;
hate less, love more;
and all good things are yours."
- Swedish Proverb

Leadership is
a potent combination
of strategy
and character.

But if you
must be without one,
be without the strategy.

- Norman Schwarzkopf

CHAPTER 4

Ten-Fold Leadership

In 1988, General H. Norman Schwarzkopf was
appointed Commander-in-Chief of the U.S. Army's Central
Command. In this capacity, he prepared a detailed plan for the
defense of the oil fields of the Persian Gulf against a
hypothetical invasion by Iraq, and it was that plan that served
as a basis for the First Gulf War, also known as *Operation
Desert Storm*. Given his reputation as a brilliant strategist, it
seems noteworthy that he would consider strategy second in
importance to character. And yet, his writings and speeches
generally emphasize character as the paramount ingredient for
successful and effective leadership.

General Dwight Eisenhower became President of the
United States in 1953 in large part because of his proven ability as
a military leader. During World War II, he served as Supreme
Commander of the Allied forces in Europe, and was responsible

for planning and supervising the successful invasion of France and Germany in 1944–45. Leading soldiers under those circumstances certainly took remarkable leadership, and Eisenhower was a masterful leader.

The U.S. Army recognizes the need for great leaders in the overall mission of winning America's wars. And they make a concerted, calculated effort to teach leadership as a skill to every member of their ranks. At the US Military Academy at West Point, cadets can major in Leadership, and every cadet is required to take at least one class in Leadership. In fact, the entire curriculum, indeed the entire culture, is focused on a mission of developing each cadet into a "leader of character". But the Army also develops the leadership skills of the enlisted soldiers and the officers who never attended the Academy.

From 2005-2007, I was personally involved in a project to develop an online leadership development tool for the U.S. Army. That tool was designed to help every employee of the U.S. Army – officers, enlisted personnel, and civilian employees - develop their own skills in leadership. I have found the Army's commitment to leadership development both inspiring and educational, and I believe every organization can benefit from improving the leadership skills of the people who work there. I believe that an organization can only be as good as its leadership, which is why I've dedicated this chapter to exploring the implementation of the Ten-Fold concept in your leadership strategies. And I use examples of Ten-Fold Leadership that I have learned from the Army leaders with whom it has been my privilege to work.

I begin with a story about a truly gifted leader I knew in Iraq, who lead me to accomplish more than I ever imagined I could, under the most trying conditions I have ever endured. And he did it (though he may not have realized it at the time) by doing good for someone else and getting it back tenfold.

Christmas Day, 2003. Balad, Iraq

First, let me explain how it was that I found myself in Iraq in the first place. I am definitely not a soldier, nor an adventurer. I'm just an ordinary person whose life has taken a few extraordinary turns. And many of those turns were the result of my husband's job with the U.S. Defense Department. Don worked as a Quality Assurance Specialist for the Defense Department – a civilian employee who served as the government's representative in factories all over the world where products were manufactured for the U.S. Military. Because these factories exist all over the United States and overseas, we spent our lives moving. Every time we moved, I was looking for a job. And every time we moved overseas, I was looking for a job on the U.S. Military base that we were assigned to.

In 2001, Don's job took us to Wiesbaden, Germany, where I eventually took a job as an IT Specialist, fixing computers and running a helpdesk for the Army. Then, in February of 2003, the war started, and my unit deployed. My security clearance had been delayed in the post-9/11 crack-down, so I couldn't deploy with them. But in July 2003, my clearance arrived, and I joined them at Camp Anaconda in Balad, Iraq.

The next 6 months would prove to be the most horrible-wonderful experience of my life.

Our unit was the supply battalion for the whole Iraq effort. As our general put it, if a soldier in Iraq wore it, ate it, drank it, drove it, fueled his vehicle with it, … in short, if a soldier in Iraq touched it, and God didn't put it there, the 3RD COSCOM put it there.

My section was the communications section of the COSCOM. Our main mission during the war was to keep the general's email working, and that wasn't easy. Electricity was iffy at best, and the heat and dust were constantly at odds with all the computers on the network. So we stayed busy just keeping the basic network systems functioning, and that was our primary focus. But because we were a headquarters, we also had Video Tele Conferencing capability – or **VTC** . The general and his staff used VTCs to communicate with his superiors in Washington and elsewhere around the globe.

While our primary mission was to provide communications for the general, we also served a side mission in support of the everyday soldier. We managed a small "internet café", which consisted of two laptop computers with access to a very slow, very unstable internet connection. Soldiers from all over would spend hours on their days off, standing in line for their 15 minutes of internet time, so they could check email and catch some news from home. Some days, the line would stretch the entire length of the building, with soldiers hoping to connect with someone back home. I knew of no soldier in those early days in Iraq who wouldn't happily trade a day's rations for a long newsy email from home. While the internet café wasn't our primary mission, keeping those two laptops running became really important to us as a unit, because we could see how important it was to the soldiers we served.

By mid-fall, we began to use the VTC equipment to coordinate video conferences between regular soldiers and their families back home. You can't imagine how heartwarming it is to put a soldier, who hasn't seen his family for a year, in a room with a TV, where he can talk face to face with his family. It is the most rewarding, inspiring thing I've ever done, to help a soldier connect face to face with his spouse, or his parents, or his children. I was especially moved when that soldier was a young woman, separated from her husband, parents, siblings, and children, as I had been, for so many long months. And I am enormously grateful for the opportunity I had to help those soldiers connect. It's the most gratifying feeling in the world – *when it worked.*

But about a third of them failed.

My coworkers and I would set up the VTCs and coordinate them with other tech specialists along the chain. Because the VTC was on a secure network, there was no direct link from us to the families in the states. So we would link up our system with a system in Baghdad, and from there it might link to Kuwait, and then to Turkey, and then to Germany, and then to Washington, and from there to an Army facility somewhere in Texas or Iowa or wherever.

We'd bring the soldier to the VTC at the appointed time, and his family would arrive at their secure VTC location – sometimes many hours from their homes – for a chance to spend six minutes with their loved one in Iraq. The families always arrived dressed in their Sunday dress best. The kids would be scoured and polished, and the little girls often sported yellow ribbons in their hair.

We would coach the soldier about the process, explaining that we had to be very strict about the six minute time limit, to assure that each soldier who has been scheduled will be able to complete his VTC in the time we have. And one of us would stand by with a stop watch and warn him as his time was running out. The soldiers were always very cooperative and would say their goodbyes and I love yous, and then they always thanked us for making it happen. It was absolute ecstasy when it worked, but it was devastating when it failed. And it failed often and for a number of reasons.

The VTC network included so many hops, and each of those hops was in a different time zone. A technician had to be present at each of the hops to accept the feed and move it along to the next hop. And that technician had to have the technical knowledge and the appropriate security clearance to access the network. Any one of the hops might fail. Sometimes there was a technical failure, or confusion about the time zones. Sometimes, the technician failed to get the memo, and sometimes he called in sick or had a more pressing mission to attend to. Sometimes electricity failed, or the network would crash. Sometimes someone would oversleep. The point is that we understood that, for all our good intentions and effort, a third of our VTCs would fail, and that would be devastating to us and especially to the soldiers and families who had been promised a visit. The spouses, parents, and children back home, dressed up and squirming with anticipation, who had driven for hours to visit with their soldier, would be crushed, and there would be nothing anyone could do to stop it.

Well, it was coming up toward Christmas and my boss, MAJ Perez, decided that we should run the VTCs all day long on Christmas Day. "We can run VTCs around the clock. At six minutes each, we can do 10 every hour. That would mean 240 soldiers who could be with their families on Christmas Day. " He was really excited about the idea, and most of my coworkers agreed it was a wonderful idea. But I went to his office to protest.

"Sir", I said, "You know that these things fail all the time, and you know how heartbreaking that is. If we attempt 240 on Christmas Day, we can count on 80 families having their hearts broken – on Christmas Day. I understand wanting to do this, but I want nothing to do with bringing about that kind of disappointment on Christmas Day. With all due respect, Sir, we just can't do that."

We had a pretty heated debate about it. (One advantage of being a civilian: I could argue with the boss.) But in the end, he was the boss, and I spent most of Christmas Day with a stopwatch in my hand, ushering soldiers, and basking in their delight as they gazed upon the faces of their families back home.

It was great. All day long, we ran soldiers – men and women, officers and enlisteds – through the process so they could spend six precious minutes with their families back home. It was a wonderful Christmas.

But then it failed. It was just after dinner, and we had just finished with a unit of Reservists from Des Moines, Iowa, when we attempted to hook up with a unit from Fort Hood, Texas.

I sat the first soldier down in the chair. He had already been coached about the process. And one of my colleagues was trying to dial in the VTC tech in Texas. But Texas wasn't answering. Every hop along the path had responded, until it got to Fort Hood, and there it was just dead air. Apparently, the technician either failed to come in, or he had some technical problem that prevented it from working. We were stuck, and I had to tell that guy that he wasn't going to see his family after all. And they weren't going to see him. He was crushed, and angry, as you can imagine, and I could only imagine the devastated look on the faces of the wife and children in Texas.

I apologized to the soldier, and went to report the failure to MAJ Perez. "Sir, Fort Hood's not answering. It appears the tech never came in."

And then MAJ Perez sprung into action. He got on the phone. It wasn't your standard phone, of course, but being in the communications department, MAJ Perez had access to all the cool toys. He called the MP station at Fort Hood, and spoke to the unfortunate soldier who had to man the switchboard on Christmas Day. He explained the situation, and asked the soldier to contact the technician at home, and tell him to get to the base and do his job.

"Sir, with all due respect, I can't do that – It's Christmas Day, Sir. That guy's a civilian, and he's at home eating turkey with his family. I can't just order him to come in."

MAJ Perez could have pulled rank and said, "This is a direct order from a superior officer." But that might not have resulted in the outcome he was after. Instead, that great leader said this:

"Son, I know it's Christmas Day. And I know that fellow is at home enjoying a turkey with his family. But we have hundreds of soldiers over here who haven't seen their families in over a year. They would love to be spending this Christmas Day eating turkey with their families.

"But they are over here in Iraq, fighting and dying for that guy's right to eat turkey with his family. Now I can't imagine that there is anything that American would rather do today than to help these soldiers visit with their families. Please call that man and give him that opportunity."

I'll never forget those words. "Please call that man and give him that opportunity." Those were some powerful words.

45 minutes later, we were back in business. The Fort Hood soldiers got to see their wives, their husbands, their little girls with yellow ribbons in their hair. And that civilian technician had a

Christmas experience he'll always treasure – maybe even his best Christmas ever.

I had seen Schwarzkopf's ideals of leadership in action. It really was all about character. And I had experienced Ten-Fold Leadership in its purest form. MAJ Perez was doing something good for those soldiers in Iraq, and because of that, he was able to garner the unquestioning cooperation and service of so many people along the chain. We all wanted to help him accomplish this for the soldiers. We all wanted to do our best to make it happen, and we all went the extra mile because it was the right thing to do. When we witnessed his desire to do that good deed, we saw MAJ Perez as a worthy, righteous leader of character, and we gave him everything we had. That's the essence of Ten-Fold Leadership, and it is as powerful in business as it was in Iraq.

Do the right thing, and your team will always respect you. People are naturally driven to support the people they respect. They'll work harder, sacrifice more, complain less, and produce better results for a leader they respect. And nothing builds respect like a kind, generous and genuine heart.

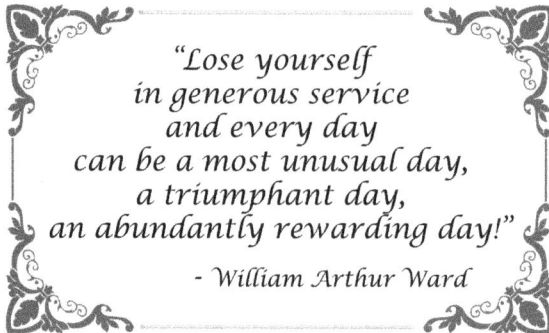

> *"Lose yourself*
> *in generous service*
> *and every day*
> *can be a most unusual day,*
> *a triumphant day,*
> *an abundantly rewarding day!"*
>
> *- William Arthur Ward*

Ten-Fold Leadership Tithing

This section isn't about dropping 10% of your income in the collection plate at church; it's about tithing in a different context. In this section, I discuss the value of tithing your efforts toward becoming a more effective leader. Perhaps you, like many successful business leaders, recognize the value of providing outstanding customer service, and you focus your efforts on achieving that goal. As a Ten-Fold marketer, you know that serving your customers well will come back to you in the form of additional sales, word-of-mouth referrals, and loyal customers. But in this section, I want you to think about how you can focus your efforts – at least 10% of your efforts – on serving your employees well.

As a business leader, you have to spend a certain amount of your time managing employees and helping them do their jobs. It's been said that the job of a great manager is to hire good people and help them do their jobs. And while helping your people accomplish their mission is an important role, that's not the role addressed by Ten-Fold Tithing. The manager who embraces Ten-Fold Tithing will commit at least 10% of the time they spend taking care of customers to the task of taking care of their own people. Since almost all of your time is consumed directly or indirectly by tasks associated with taking care of customers, I want you to consider the value of spending 10% of that time actually taking care of your own people.

When you work with an employee to help them do their job better, they appreciate it and they perform better because of it. But when you spend time taking care of your employees as human beings, that's when you really reap the Ten-Fold rewards.

I had a great boss once who managed a team of 8 employees. Every Wednesday, she took one of us to lunch. She paid for the meal, but the real value to me wasn't the cost of a sandwich and fries; it was the conversation we had over lunch. She made it a point to let me do most of the talking, and she asked me questions that allowed me to really open up. It was a brilliant strategy, and one I encourage you to emulate.

She would ask me about my family and what challenges I was facing outside of work. The fact that she cared enough to ask was important, and I appreciated her taking the interest. It also gave her a greater understanding of what motivates me and what is important to me. Over the course of a year, she and I would have several such conversations, and each one brought her to a closer understanding of how to manage, lead and motivate me.

She would also ask about my challenges at work. Sometimes she would have a simple solution for a problem I was having. Other times, the solution wasn't as readily available, but just sharing the problem helped me cope with it. She would ask me for suggestions for improving our processes and our work environment, and asked my opinion about issues that affected my job. Knowing that she genuinely respected my opinion was very motivational to me. I found myself wanting to please her, to earn her respect, and to help her succeed.

With a team of eight employees, my boss was able to schedule a lunch with each of us every couple of months. We each had the same opportunity to bend her ear, have our say, and share our ideas. We all looked forward to our "Lunch with the Boss", and I'm sure she enjoyed them too. But more importantly, those lunches created a bond between us that enhanced our professional relationship and allowed us each to grow and develop under her leadership. And those lunches cost her just a few bucks and a few hours each month.

She used those lunches as an opportunity to care for us as human beings, listening to our concerns and our ideas, and offering solutions when possible. It was a simple strategy, easily implemented, that paid huge dividends. She was definitely a Ten-Fold leader.

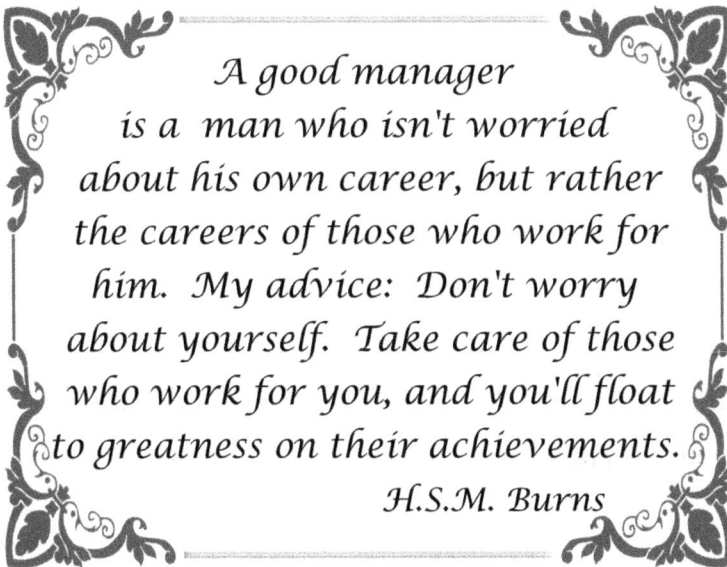

> *A good manager is a man who isn't worried about his own career, but rather the careers of those who work for him. My advice: Don't worry about yourself. Take care of those who work for you, and you'll float to greatness on their achievements.*
> *H.S.M. Burns*

There are many ways for a business leader to take care of his people, and I want you to get creative and implement a plan that will help you take care of your people. A raise or a bonus is always nice, and your people will certainly appreciate either one, especially if they know you had to work hard to get it for them. Awards are especially nice because they not only show your appreciation for the employee's efforts, but also show you are willing to put in the time to get them the award. Nothing motivates like appreciation, and if it requires effort on your part, it's even more motivating.

Take the time to recognize your employee's special days. "Today's you daughter's birthday, right?" A greeting like that will always be appreciated, and if you can add, "Why don't you go home a little early", you'll be a real hero. All the special dates should be in your calendar so when you turn on your computer in the morning, you get a reminder. It's simple, effective, and always appreciated. And it will come back to you tenfold.

Never underestimate the importance of pets in your employees' lives. Nothing will turn an employee against you faster than showing disregard for their beloved pets. If someone needs time off for a vet appointment, you should definitely grant it, and do so with understanding and concern. When he returns, be sure to ask about Fluffy's wellbeing. And if Fluffy dies, be prepared to support your employee through whatever grieving time he needs. Recognize that he may not be as focused and effective while he's grieving, and let him know you're aware of what he's going through.

When you embrace the concept of Ten-Fold Tithing, you will spend as much as 10% of your work life taking care of your own people, investing in them and making them happy. Spend time thinking about their challenges and how you can alleviate them. Find ways to bolster their confidence, and self-esteem. Help them advance professionally, and encourage them to seek new opportunities. Ten-Fold Tithing might require a shift in your priorities, and it will almost certainly result in some scheduling changes. After all, in a 40 hour week, 10% is a full 4 hours. But if you will invest 10% of your work effort in taking care of your people, I am confident they'll invest 100% of their work effort helping you. And when your team is truly motivated to helping you and your business succeed, amazing things can happen. Productivity improves, turnover decreases, and stress levels drop throughout the organization. And it's all reflected in the bottom line. That's the magic of Ten-Fold Leadership, and it's part of the systemic approach to Ten-Fold Marketing.

Hire the best.
Pay them fairly.
Communicate frequently.
Provide challenges and rewards.
Believe in them.
Get out of their way
and they'll knock your socks off.
- Mary Ann Allison

Anita Roddick, was a British businesswoman, a human rights activist and an avid environmentalist. She's probably best known as the founder of *The Body Shop*, one of the first cosmetics companies to prohibit the use of ingredients tested on animals, and one of the first to promote fair trade with third world countries. Deeply impressed by Roddick's character and ethics, Queen Elizabeth II appointed her a Dame Commander of the Order of the British Empire in 2003. While that title certainly has its privileges, it's Roddick's business strategies that have most defined her life and her legacy. Her customers happily paid a premium for her company's products, knowing that the company held those lofty standards relating to animal cruelty and human rights. But Roddick's motives weren't entirely about profits either. As she explained, "I want to work for a company that contributes to and is part of the community. I want something not just to invest in. I want something to believe in."

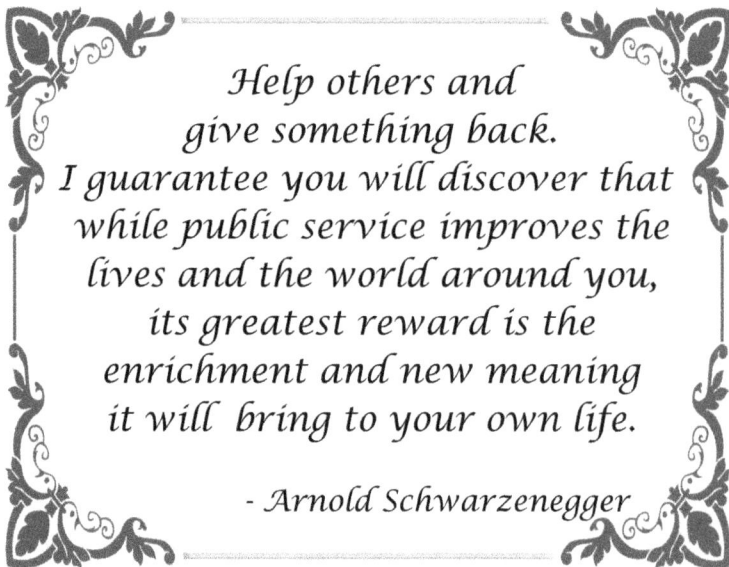

Help others and give something back. I guarantee you will discover that while public service improves the lives and the world around you, its greatest reward is the enrichment and new meaning it will bring to your own life.

- Arnold Schwarzenegger

We make a living
by what we get,
but we make a life
by what we give.

- Winston Churchill

CHAPTER 5
Your Ten-Fold Company

Ben & Jerry's is a company that fully understood and embraced the Ten-Fold concept, though they didn't call it that at the time. Both of the original partners had an innate desire to do good, to be generous, to behave ethically and morally, and to serve the greater good. They put their money, and their leadership to good use, in service to their customers, their community, the planet, and their fellow man. And the results have been remarkable. Their support of the many causes they fostered has been well documented, and the effect they had on those causes is immeasurable. But the story I find most remarkable, and the one I want you to take to heart, is the effect that those causes have had on their corporate identity, their public image, and their bottom line. It seems that they had discovered the amazing truth that Ben Sweetland espoused in his inspiring book, *I Can! the Key to Life's*

Golden Secrets, "We cannot hold a torch to light another's path without brightening our own."

So how can you put that truth to work in your own company? How can you create a Ten-Fold culture within your own organization? I think the answer is as individual as you are, but the fact that you're reading this book is an indication that you are on the right path.

3 Steps to Your Ten-Fold Company

Step 1: Believe it.

You first must embrace and acknowledge the power of selfless service. A lot of very successful people have embraced the Ten-Fold concept, and it has helped them achieve even greater success. Obviously, the founders of Ben & Jerry's embraced it. Another pertinent example is Oprah Winfrey, arguably America's most successful woman, and also one of our most celebrated philanthropists. Her entire public history is filled with examples of selfless service and charitable giving. She believes that giving is a necessary component of a joyful, successful life.

In 1997, on an episode of *The Oprah Winfrey Show,* Oprah asked her viewers to join her in working to improve the lives of others. She asked them to collect spare change for 150 scholarships that would be distributed through the Boys & Girls Clubs. She also asked that they volunteer their time to help build 200 homes with Habitat for Humanity. The response was immense and thousands of Oprah fans stepped up to help with their time, their spare change and more. That was the beginning of the international charity known today as Oprah's Angel Network.

Using her money, her connections, and her influence, Oprah has had an enormous impact on the lives of thousands of people. And Oprah's Angel Network has created opportunities, especially for impoverished women and children, across America and around the world. With the support of this charity, over 50 schools have been built in underdeveloped nations. Thousands of children have been provided with shoes, clothing and school supplies totaling over a million dollars. As part of the Hurricane Katrina and Rita recovery efforts, nearly 300 homes were built or restored. And dozens of organizations around the world have been aided in their missions to help the underprivileged, and under-resourced citizens of the world. The list of Oprah's contributions seems endless, and the results have been unparalleled.

At this stage of her life, Oprah's most limited resource is certainly her time. And yet, she continues to give freely of that precious commodity as well. And it seems that the more she gives away, the more she gets back. She wasn't always rich and successful, but with hard work, brains, and a commitment to doing what's right, Oprah has brought success upon herself. As she says, "What I know for sure is that what you give comes back to you." That's Ten-Fold Marketing at its best!

Just listen to these powerful words of advice:

"I've come to believe that each of us has a personal calling that's as unique as a fingerprint - and that the best way to succeed is to discover what you love and then find a way to offer it to others in the form of service, working hard, and also allowing the energy of the universe to lead you. "

Oprah Winfrey, *O Magazine, September 2002*

Ben and Jerry believe it. Oprah believes it. Successful people from every profession, in every part of the world, across the ages have believed it. And that great author and mentor, Jim Rohn, believed it when he said, "Whoever renders service to many puts himself in line for greatness -- great wealth, great return, great satisfaction, great reputation, and great joy." Believing in the power of Ten-Fold Marketing is the first step to realizing its potential.

Step 2: Plan It.

The next step in creating your Ten-Fold company is planning and setting goals. As Yogi Berra so aptly put it, "If you don't know where you are going, you might wind up someplace else." So think about how you would like to position your company as a Ten-Fold company, and make a plan for getting there. What is your vision for the good your company can achieve? What causes do you care about most? What charities focus their efforts on the issues you see as most critical? What volunteer activities can you and your team members do in your own community that will affect the people you want to help? And how will your service be accomplished? But first, I suggest you look closer to home, and start planning your Ten-Fold company from the inside out.

Charity begins at home.

In 2010, Crain's New York Business, a major business publication, listed a young company called ZocDoc as the best place to work in New York City. ZocDoc is a free service for patients that helps them find a local doctor that fits their needs and instantly book an appointment online, usually to take place within 24 – 72 hours. If you've ever had a problem or long wait getting in to see a medical specialist, you'll appreciate how valuable that service can be. In fact, it was exactly that scenario that gave rise to the idea for ZocDoc. A young entrepreneur, Cyrus Massoumi, had ruptured an eardrum on a flight, and couldn't find a doctor for four days. He knew that there had to be an easier way for patients to find and book appointments with doctors, and that was when he came up with the idea for ZocDoc. In doing research for this book, I spoke with Massoumi, the CEO and Founder of ZocDoc, about his business and his Ten-Fold Marketing. He was unbelievably gracious and generous with his time, and he shared with me some of the strategies that have made ZocDoc not only a great place to work, but also one of the fastest growing businesses in America today. As Massoumi explained, "One of those strategies has been to always place the employees' needs ahead of the boss's. And in return, they give us amazing work every day."

A visit to the ZocDoc website is itself an education in Ten-Fold Marketing. If you visit the company's "We're Hiring" page, you'll see some of the things that make this the best place to work in New York City. They tout great benefits (healthcare, naturally, and a 401K plan), but they also offer, "Delicious, healthy catered lunch every day" and "The opportunity to reach out and help your fellow citizens by doing what you do best!" They also include this Ten-Fold tidbit: "Our strategy: combine smart people, hard work and just a tiny bit of karaoke."

ZocDoc hires great people, which is made easier by the fact that they are such a great place to work, and then they help those great employees succeed and be happy. Clearly, the leaders at ZocDoc are the servants of their employees, and that's a strategy that has worked well for them. When we spoke, Massoumi said they were looking to hire 10 people per week and they expect to be nationwide soon.

The list of investors that have helped to finance that sensational growth is a real testament to their Ten-Fold philosophy. Some of those investors include Jeff Bezos (Founder of Amazon), Goldman Sachs, and DST Global, whose investments also include Facebook, Groupon, and Twitter. ZocDoc is yet another example of a company whose commitments to kindness, generosity, and selfless service toward their own employees have resulted in remarkable, perhaps even "tenfold" success.

Expand from the core, outward to the customer.

Cyrus Massoumi taught me a great deal about the strategies that he feels are responsible for the ZocDoc success, and the one that he holds most scared is one of their core values: Patients First.

"We stress that in every interaction, the patient is #1, ahead of ourselves," he said. "Employees are ahead of the boss, and the patient is ahead of everyone."

He told me they work very hard to create customer loyalty through fulfillment and satisfaction.

"For example," he explained, "if a patient makes an appointment [through ZocDoc] and the doctor has to reschedule it, we reach out to that customer. We'll do something for them like give them a gift certificate to Amazon."

It's important to note that, in that example, it was the doctor, and not ZocDoc who was responsible for the inconvenience to the patient. But At ZocDoc, they recognize the value of truly exceptional customer care, and they are serious about putting the patient ahead of themselves. For them, a cancelled appointment is an opportunity for them to shine. The patient doesn't expect it, because the patient knows it wasn't ZocDoc's fault.

Customer service gets a lot of lip service in America, but there are few companies that embrace true service as well as ZocDoc does. Massoumi is certain that customer service is a major component in the success his company has enjoyed. So as you plan the strategy that will build your Ten-Fold company, be sure you put selfless service to your customers at the very core of that strategy.

Move your thinking beyond the idea of customer satisfaction, and focus your efforts on total, unparalleled customer delight. People expect customer satisfaction. You need to give them something they don't expect – something so extraordinary that they'll be amazed by it, and tell their friends about it. Customer service in a Ten-Fold company isn't about giving the customer what they paid for; it's about true generosity and selfless service. Plan your Ten-Fold company around that concept and success will follow.

Go beyond the customer, to the community and the world.

Charity begins at home, which is why I suggested that you start your Ten-Fold planning with generosity and caring for your own employees, and then expand it to include the customers that pay your bills. With those plans in place, you can now begin to plan for the Ten-Fold strategies that will reach beyond your company and touch people in your community, and beyond. I'll talk more about that in Chapter Seven, where I help you identify the focus for your giving strategies.

Step 3: Achieve it.

Once your vision is defined, it's time to act, and this is where a lot of good intentions fall to the wayside. The trouble is that implementing a plan for volunteerism or corporate giving usually requires some tedious administrative work, and no one seems to have the time or the motivation to attend to those details. So I will share with you some words of wisdom I read years ago, by a man who authored a number of popular books about parenting and child rearing. Fitzhugh Dodson gave parents across America this advice, "First you write down your goal; your second job is to break down your goal into a series of steps, beginning with steps which are absurdly easy." Those words provide sound advice for you as a business leader too, and are echoed by life coaches and business consultants every day. One of the most brilliant minds in leadership consulting today is Michael Hyatt, the Chairman of Thomas Nelson Publishers, the largest Christian publishing company in the world and the seventh largest trade book publishing company in the U.S. On his personal blog (michaelhyatt.com), he states, "My philosophy is that if you are going to lead well, you must be thoughtful and purposeful about it." And according to Hyatt, that begins with writing down your goals.

So commit your giving goals to writing, break them down into steps, beginning with those "absurdly easy" ones, and then assign the steps of your plan to the appropriate team members, and hold each person accountable for accomplishing them. We'll talk more about this in Chapter 8. For now, just realize that the tasks may be simple or challenging; they may be interesting or tedious. But they will have to be done if you are going to accomplish your vision for a Ten-Fold company. Somehow, you will have to take the lead and motivate your team to get things done.

The three steps to creating your Ten-Fold company are simple, and the rewards are immense. BELIEVE IT, like Ben Cohen and Jerry Greenfield believed it. PLAN IT, from the inside out, like the founder of ZocDoc did. And then ACHIEVE IT, in a way that will be uniquely your own.

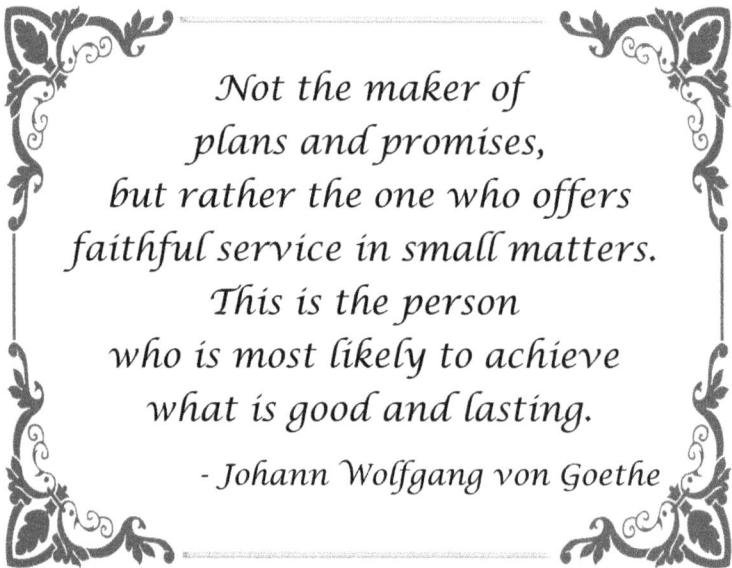

> *Not the maker of*
> *plans and promises,*
> *but rather the one who offers*
> *faithful service in small matters.*
> *This is the person*
> *who is most likely to achieve*
> *what is good and lasting.*
>
> *- Johann Wolfgang von Goethe*

Part Three

Your Ten-Fold Strategy

Give what you have.

To someone,
it may be better
than you
dare think.

- Henry Wadsworth Longfellow

CHAPTER 6

Identifying Your Assets

Step one in creating your Ten-Fold company is to BELIEVE IT. I hope that the previous pages have helped you do that, but if you ever doubt that Ten-Fold Marketing works, just think about Ben & Jerry's. If two guys from northern Vermont could make a fortune in the ice cream business, surely you and I can gain success in our own industries by following the shining example they have set for us. I believe it, and if you do too, we can move on with your vision for your own Ten-Fold company.

Step two is the fundamentally important step in which you will PLAN IT. In fact, this step is so critically important, I've dedicated the next four chapters to helping you develop a plan that will propel your Ten-Fold Marketing success. In this chapter, I focus on helping you identify your assets, because you may have resources that you don't realize can be shared. In Chapter 7, I talk about who you can share those resources with, and in Chapter 8, I help you formulate the plan that will maximize the impact on both the recipients of your generosity, and on your Ten-Fold business. Then, in Chapter 9, I focus on the most important focus of any successful business – the customer.

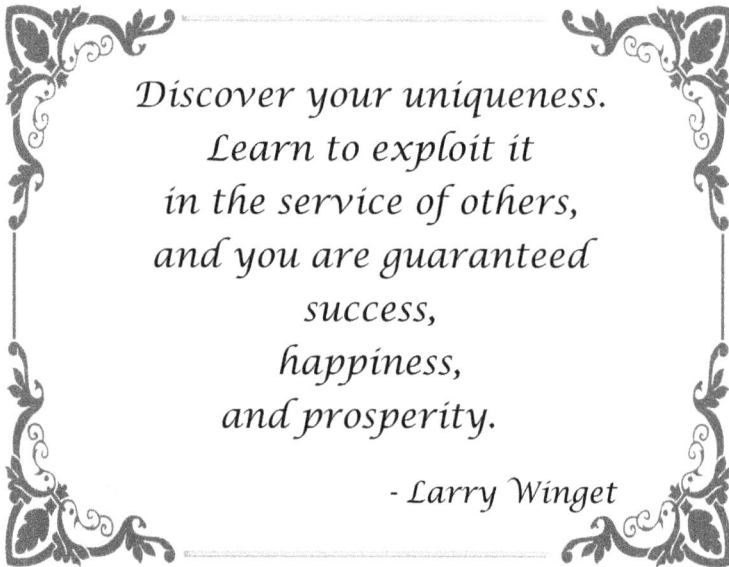

Discover your uniqueness.
Learn to exploit it
in the service of others,
and you are guaranteed
success,
happiness,
and prosperity.

- Larry Winget

If you're like most of the small business owners I know, you don't have a lot of money to donate to charity. But money is an asset that can have a tremendous impact on a Ten-Fold Marketing strategy, so I want you to think about investing some of your cold hard cash in your acts of kindness. The beautiful thing about money is its flexibility. With cash, you can give when and where the need is greatest, or where it can have the most impact, or where it will produce the most immediate results. You have lots of other assets, and we'll talk about those shortly, but first, let's talk about ways to invest some good old-fashioned greenbacks in your Ten-Fold Marketing, because as the saying goes, "Money Talks!"

Ben Cohen and Jerry Greenfield understood the value of cash in their charitable giving, and they made it a cornerstone of their Ten-Fold company. Early on, long before they were a household name, Ben & Jerry's were committed to giving 10% of their profits to charity. It's a simple strategy, one that any business could easily implement. The percentage of profits remains constant, but the actual dollar amount will grow and shrink, as your profits grow and shrink. In good months (or years, depending on how it works best for your company), your charitable giving increases, but if your company hits a slump, or the economy takes a downturn, you charitable donations fall off accordingly. Also, the donations are based on after-expenses profits, so your company's investments in people or equipment come first, and your charitable giving is based on the amount of profit you realize after those expenses.

One of the advantages in taking this approach is the pure simplicity of implementing it. It's simply a percentage of the money you make, after taxes and other expenses are taken out. Bigger profits reap bigger donations. It's insanely simple.

Another advantage in this plan is that you are never committed to a specific dollar amount, and that can be a big deal for small businesses for whom cash flow can be a constant challenge. It avoids the unfortunate scenario in which a company makes a pledge of support, and then must renege because the cash isn't available. In a Ten-Fold Marketing strategy, that's one scenario that will backfire big time.

There are other strategies for coming up with cash for your charitable giving, and most of us have used one or more of these strategies at some point in our lives. Just think about how you saved up money to buy that first bicycle or stereo, when you were a kid. Here are just a few ideas that I've seen work for both kids and adults, and that I know can work for you, as you strive to allocate money to your Ten-Fold Marketing plan.

- **Pay yourself first.** Dave Ramsey and a lot of other financial coaches advocate this as a great saving strategy. Out of every paycheck, take a dollar, or ten dollars, or a hundred dollars – whatever is appropriate for your own situation - and put it in savings. "Save it first, and you'll never miss it", is the theory. I think that's a brilliant saving strategy for every man, woman and child to follow, and now I want to suggest the second step:

- **Pay your charity second**. Open a second savings account (or put another coffee can on the counter) and sock away an amount of money every week. Then that cash will be readily available when the perfect moment – the perfect need – arises.

- **Keep the change.** Empty your pocket change (or the change in your purse) every night before bed. Put it in that coffee can, and watch it add up. It's a fairly painless way to save up a few dollars a month and you'll be able to see it growing every night. One variation that I've seen work is to encourage your employees and customers to add their change to the kitty. Lots of large corporations invite their customers to donate their change, or add a donation to their bill, at the checkout counter. And lots of small businesses place the coffee can on the counter with an invitation to donate to a local charity or special cause.

- **Host an event.** Set aside a day in your calendar for a charity event.
    - o   A car wash for the local high school marching band
    - o   A walk-a-thon for the March of Dimes
    - o   A bake sale or yard sale for a local family in need
    - o   A 5K Run for the American Cancer Society

These events can bring in cash for a deserving charity, and they can be terrific for team building and employee morale, if you keep it fun and voluntary.

- **Raffle the boss.** Actually, you can raffle anything of value, but a boss raffle can be a lot of fun. I once worked for a school that raffled the principal, and one of my favorite teachers won the prize. She got to put the principal to work for an entire Saturday, doing whatever odd jobs she needed done. "I worked his butt off", she told me later. "It cost me twenty-eight bucks, and I got my lawn raked and my porch railing repaired. I even made him run the vacuum. But my favorite part was just me being his boss for a change!"

Obviously, there are countless ways for an individual or a company to raise a few bucks for charity. So have fun with it, get creative, and set aside some cash for your Ten-Fold Marketing. When the need arises, or the opportunity strikes, you'll have some money in the kitty that can be allocated at a moment's notice. And that's when the magic can happen. This was an important lesson I learned from Tory Johnson, and a story I want to share with you.

In 2010, I met Tory Johnson for the first time. Tory is a regular contributor on ABC's *Good Morning America*, and CEO of *Women for Hire*, a company that helps women succeed in the workplace. She's also the Founder and dynamo behind *Spark & Hustle*, a touring business conference for women entrepreneurs, which is where we first met. In April of 2010, *Spark & Hustle* came to Orlando, and as a wide-eyed attendee, I was impressed by Tory's natural style and accessibility.

During one of the breaks, I waited in line for an opportunity to speak to Tory in person, and when my turn came, I told her I was starting work on this book, and explained the general concept to her. My hope was that I would gain permission to contact her later for an interview, to see if she might have a Ten-Fold story that would be appropriate for inclusion in my book. But Tory did me one better! Right then and there, she told me about an experience she had personally had in which a good deed had come back to her business tenfold.

In August of 2005, America was hit with one of the most devastating natural disasters in our history, a hurricane named Katrina, that killed almost 2,000 people, and destroyed billions of dollars in property. But many who survived the initial storm surge and subsequent flooding were left homeless, jobless, and utterly hopeless.

The city hardest hit by Katrina was New Orleans, Louisiana, where the storm destroyed over 275,000 homes, and so many businesses that over 400,000 jobs were lost. Well over a million people were ordered to evacuate, but many of them were unable to do so, and tens of thousands of people were stranded on rooftops awaiting rescue. The entire nation watched in horror as the extent and severity of the disaster unfolded on television. And then Americans took action.

According to the Corporation for National and Community Service, more than half a million Americans journeyed to the Gulf Coast in the year following the disaster to volunteer in hurricane relief and recovery efforts. The figures compiled by the agency also reveal that tens of millions more people, while not traveling to the Gulf region, supported relief efforts in a variety of ways.[4] Thousands upon thousands of truckloads of food, clothing and other provisions were gathered and shipped to the region, and millions of dollars in donations were collected by the Red Cross and other relief agencies. And like so many Americans, Tory Johnson yearned to help in any way she could.

---

[4] www.nationalservice.gov

"Lots of people were working to get these people the basic necessities – food, water, a place to stay. But I had another idea. A lot of the people who had been displaced were poor working class people, who had been working at minimum wage type jobs. The Taco Bells or McDonalds where they had been working had been destroyed. They had no jobs to go back to."

So Tory packed her bags and went to Houston, where many of the displaced had been taken, and set up a sort of command post where people could go if they needed a job. She learned, for example, that Taco Bell had agreed to provide jobs at other locations for any of their current employees displaced by the storm. A young woman named Doris Banks was one of those employees.

Until the storm wiped it out, Doris Banks had been working at a Taco Bell in New Orleans and living in public housing. She was only 20 years old. Hurricane Katrina destroyed both her apartment and her workplace, and she was evacuated to Houston, where she would have to start the process of rebuilding her life. Imagine how frightening it would have been for that young woman, homeless, penniless, jobless, in a strange city, surrounded by thousands of equally desperate strangers. She had walked to a nearby Taco Bell to ask for work but was told that they had no jobs. She huddled on an Army cot in that ocean of despair, and then she saw Tory's hand-written sign that read, "Are you looking for a job?"

She gathered her strength and walked up to Tory, and learned that Taco Bell would guarantee her a job at any company-owned location. (Unfortunately, the place Doris had visited on her own the day before was a franchise – not a company-owned location.) That night, Tory printed out a list of Taco Bell locations in Houston and cross-referenced their ZIP codes with those of public housing vacancies. She found a one-bedroom unit within three blocks of a company-owned Taco Bell, and took Doris there the next morning. But when they arrived, they were told that the apartment was a condo that did not accept public housing funds.

Tory can be very persuasive, and that day, she persuaded the landlord to let Doris rent it for the $541 a month she received from the government. And she convinced him to speed up the paperwork so Doris could sign the lease that day.

Doris was stunned by Tory's generosity and her caring, but Tory wasn't finished with her yet. "Let's go shopping", she said, and took Doris to the Wal-Mart across the street from the apartment.

They spent $4,000 buying furniture, clothing, kitchen utensils and a cell phone (the bills would go to Tory). Doris Banks now had a job, a home, and the basic necessities she needed to get back on her feet.

Back in Manhattan, a New York Times columnist was working on a story about the job crisis brought on by Katrina, and she heard about Tory's trip to the Gulf Coast region. Lisa Belkin's next column told the story of Doris Banks and the help she had received from Tory Johnson. "Obviously, I hadn't expected that to happen", Tory said, "but when that interview ran in the Times, it opened some doors for me that I could never have anticipated. And some of those opportunities would never have been realized if not for my trip to the Gulf."

Tory had been moved by the plight of those hurricane survivors, and she had taken action to help them. It was a purely selfless act, and not one without substantial sacrifice on her part. But the cost of the trip, in both dollars and time away from her family and her business, was a sacrifice she felt she needed to make.

There's absolutely no doubt that it has come back to her tenfold, in both goodwill and public recognition for herself and her company. As a direct result of her generosity and caring, Tory received recognition in two different columns in the New York Times, a huge piece in the NY Post, and was given an opportunity to talk about it on Good Morning America. She received emails from appreciative and impressed strangers who read the story and wanted to be in her network. And it was all the kind of positive recognition that differentiated her from other people in the "jobs/workplace/career" space. Tory was recognized publicly as a woman who doesn't sit in an ivory tower and dispense advice. Rather, she is a woman who gets in the field and gets her hands dirty. She cares deeply about the people she serves, and she puts her time and money into that effort. But none of that recognition could have been planned or foreseen. She just saw a need and wanted to do something. As Tory has said, "I just thought if we all take one person under our wing, we can get them all out of here." So she took Doris Banks under her wing, and made a difference in that one life. Tory gained the public recognition for herself and her company, but that was never her intention, and it's her personal satisfaction in having made a genuine difference in the lives of people like Doris Banks that she sees as her greatest reward.

Obviously, Tory Johnson had the money available to help Doris Banks and the others that she worked with after the disaster. And having that cash available made a huge difference for Doris Banks. So I want you to do as I have done, and start building your war chest. Put aside a little money every week that you can use when the moment strikes and the need is at hand, because Ten-Fold Marketing requires you to be ready when opportunity strikes.

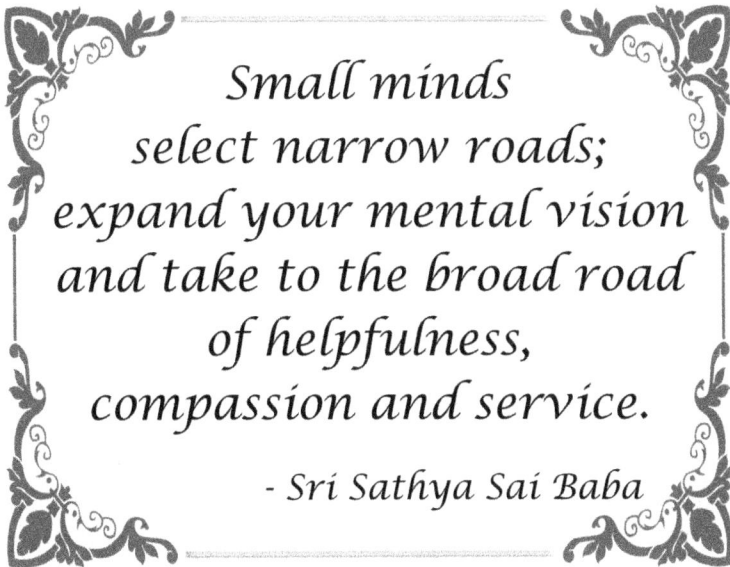

> *Small minds*
> *select narrow roads;*
> *expand your mental vision*
> *and take to the broad road*
> *of helpfulness,*
> *compassion and service.*
>
> *- Sri Sathya Sai Baba*

Cold, hard cash can be a powerful tool in your Ten-Fold Marketing strategy, and I strongly urge you to set some aside for those special unpredictable circumstances. Being in a position to give when the need is immediate will help you serve the people who need your help at the moment they need it, and doing so will maximize your impact on them, and on your Ten-Fold Marketing campaign.

While cash may be the most flexible and most liquid asset available to you, it's by no means the only asset you can use in your Ten-Fold Marketing campaign. So let's focus briefly on what other assets you might have that you can bring to the table.

Identifying Your Non-Cash Assets

The people in need, and the organizations that serve those needs are always looking for money. You have other assets that they could use as well, and you should identify what those assets are, and how you might put them to use for the charities and causes you want to help. I have found that in general, your non-cash assets will likely fall into three categories: Time, Skill, and Property. So I challenge you to think about each of those and determine which of them you could commit to your Ten-Fold Marketing campaign.

Time

You Do Have Time. I know you think you're too busy as it is, but let's get real. Whether you run a part-time home-based business, or you are the President of the United States, you have exactly 24 hours in every day. So please, face the fact that you have just as much time as anyone else. If you don't have the time to do the things that are most important to you, it's not time that's lacking. It's time management. So schedule some time – in your personal calendar, or in the work week of your employees – and give that precious commodity to the people you want to help. You can make a huge difference in the lives of the people in need, if you just schedule some time into your calendar to volunteer.

Many organizations allot a certain amount of time for their employees to volunteer in the community. Maybe you give your employees (and yourself) two days a year to volunteer for the charity of their choice. That's a concept I call "Do Good Days", and it's a cornerstone of the Ten-Fold Marketing strategy in my business and many others.

Do Good Days

I can't tell you who first envisioned the concept, but I can tell you that Do Good Days (or some variation on the theme) have become an important part of the corporate culture within many organization.

The idea is a simple one: Give people a challenge, or an opportunity to "Do Good" on company time. Some companies give their employees an amount of time (a few hours a year, for example, or a day every month) to do volunteer work within their community. This concept is one I really want you to embrace within your company, because the payoff can be monumental on so many levels.

I once knew a woman who worked for an organization that allowed every employee two days a year to volunteer for the charity of their choice, without spending any vacation days. (The woman told me that she used her free days to volunteer at her kids' school.) There were just a few basic rules that she had to follow in order to get paid for those volunteer days:

- She had to schedule it at least a week ahead of time. (That seems reasonable.)
- She had to get the boss's approval for her charity. (No, your cousin's bachelor party wouldn't get approval, but almost any actual volunteerism would.)
- She was expected to wear a name badge or t-shirt with the company's logo on it while she was there volunteering. (This gave the company some recognition for their involvement in the community.)
- She had to bring in photos of herself on the job site, and those photos would be posted in the employee lounge.

That last rule was sheer genius, I believe. First, it provided some proof that the employee actually did volunteer that day. But those photos provided so much more than that. Those pictures allowed the employees to share that aspect of their personal lives, which had a very positive impact on the workplace. As the bulletin board filled up with pictures of volunteering, the employees began to appreciate the company's (and their own) impact on the community. They took pride in being part of such a positive team, and such a generous company. And they came to understand a little more about the things that their coworkers cared deeply about.

This lady spent her days at her children's school, but other employees spent their "Do Good Days" volunteering at the local animal shelter, the public library, the food bank, the women's shelter, or the Girl Scouts cookie drive. That bulletin board filled up with pictures of smiling employees, serving their community, helping their chosen charities, and being supported in their efforts by the company that cared about them and their causes.

Doing Good as a Team

A special bond often develops between colleagues and coworkers who participate in Do Good Days together. This is one reason some companies have embraced the idea of the Company-Wide Do Good Day. Some companies choose a charity and spend a day volunteering together for that one charity. You might find the entire workforce of a company working together on a Habitat for Humanity work site, or organizing a "Race for the Cure" event. When an entire team of people come together for a day of volunteering, they can have a big impact on the charity that day. It can also have a big impact on the members of that team, and on the company at large.

Think about ways your own company could impact the community if you all took a single day and worked together to make a real difference. This is one of my favorite Ten-Fold ideas. Turn out the lights, lock the doors, and let's go build a house! Set the telephone answering machine's message to say, "Thank you for calling the XYZ Corporation. We're sorry to have missed your call, but today is a special day at XYZ. Today, our entire company is volunteering to help build a house for Habitat for Humanity. If you have an emergency, please call Ms. Jones on her cell at 555-555-5555. She'll put down her hammer and get you the help you need. If it's not an emergency, please leave a message and we'll call you back tomorrow."

Whether it's accomplished by a number of individuals, or as a team, this is one simple, yet highly effective way to donate a valuable asset – time – to your Ten-Fold Marketing campaign, and plant the seeds that will eventually reap your Ten-Fold successes. Now let's talk about some other non-cash assets. Let's talk about your skills.

Skills, Knowledge and Expertise.

You and your team members have skills and expertise that can help lots of people in need and the organizations that help them. So consider what skills you may have and how you might put them to use for your Ten-Fold Marketing campaign. If you are in a service industry, consider donating your services to one or more charitable organizations in your community. Attorneys, accountants, doctors, even web designers, frequently take on pro bono clients, and you can too. You'll need to set some limits, but this can be a great way to do what you do best for the benefit of a deserving charity or civic organization.

But what if you own a coffee shop or a book store? What skills do you have that you could put to use for your favorite charity? Well, that depends upon the charity, and their specific needs, but there are certain skills that you, as a business owner have that almost every charitable organization can use. Could you train some of their volunteers to better use a computer? Could you teach them how to organize their files (either paper or digital)? Maybe you have a creative flair and could help them design some flyers or brochures. Maybe you could help them organize or promote their next event or fundraiser. Depending on what the organization (or the individual) needs, you almost certainly have skills or special expertise that can help. Whatever expertise you bring to the table, you can find people and charities that need it. It's just a matter of matching their need with your capabilities, and putting your skills expertise, and knowledge to work for a good cause.

Got Stuff?

Everybody has stuff they don't need, stuff they can't use, or stuff they no longer want, and that's a non-cash asset you should definitely put to use for your Ten-Fold Marketing campaign. Again, depending on the person or charity you want to help, you may have a little or a lot of stuff that they can use. If you are in a retail business, you may want to consider donating some of your products to a good cause, or identify specific items in your inventory that will be sold specifically to benefit your chosen charity.

All retail and service businesses occasionally find they have office supplies or furniture that they no longer need, and charities are often happy to receive those donations. Even junk cars and unwanted time-share properties can be donated, and there are hundreds of charities willing to accept those as well.

Depending upon who you have chosen to help, you may find that you have other "stuff" that they need, or that they can sell for cash. Work with your chosen charity to determine their needs and what you can do to best meet some of those needs.

In many cases, your donations are tax-deductible, so be sure to talk with your accountant about that, and get receipts when you make your donations.

The important thing to remember, as you work to identify the assets you can contribute to your chosen cause, is that every little bit helps, and half a loaf is better than no bread. Give what you can and be creative in finding new assets that can make a difference in your community.

> *"No act of kindness,*
> *no matter how small,*
> *is ever wasted.*
>
> *- Aesop*

I slept
and dreamt that
life was joy.

I awoke
and saw that
life is service.

I acted
and behold,
service was joy.

- Rabindranath Tagore

CHAPTER 7
Identifying Your Focus

T his may be the most enjoyable (and perhaps the most debated) step in creating your Ten-Fold Marketing campaign – identifying the focus of your giving. This is the point where you consider all the causes that are most important to you, and choose the one (or the few) that will receive the benefit from the campaign you're about to launch.

Large corporations may choose several causes to embrace and support, but smaller businesses will likely want to choose one or two that will be their primary focus. I have found that many small business owners choose a charity that has a strong personal relevance in their lives. For some, a family member has been stricken by cancer or another devastating disease, so they are committed to helping find a cure or a better treatment for that particular disease. If this is the case with you, options are available for you to get involved, either through volunteerism or through donations of cash and other real or personal property.

Other small business leaders choose to help where the need is the greatest in terms of human suffering, such as world hunger or human trafficking. Some are compelled to serve abandoned or abused animals, or local foster children, or battered women, or homeless vets, or other local charities that seek to ease the suffering of the least empowered among us. If these are the charities that speak to your heart, there are hundreds of organizations throughout the nation and around the world working to facilitate that aid.

And there are thousands of other worthy causes, and new ones appearing every day. As government coffers are strained to provide greater services to more people with less money, the need for private donations and faith-based initiatives continues to grow. Today, perhaps more than ever in our history, Americans are faced with choices and decisions about their charitable contributions, and a greater need than at any time in our memory. So how do you choose?

Almost all non-profit organizations are trying to provide more assistance than ever, with fewer donations. As the economy struggles to regain its strength, and as the number of needy Americans grows, charities are having to ask their contributors to be more generous than ever. So finding a cause that will benefit from your contributions is easy. Choosing between the many worthwhile causes is the hard part. And in the end, it boils down to a personal choice for you and your team to make. If you're a one-woman business, the decision making process is simpler – Just choose the cause that feels right and commit to helping in any way you can. But if you have a team of employees and partners, the process of choosing the appropriate causes can be a lot more complicated.

If you own the business, you can simply make the choice yourself and ask your team to accept it. But I urge you to approach it differently. I strongly suggest you take the time to get input from the entire team, and make a decision that creates the greatest buy-in possible from as many team members as possible. Remember that this isn't just a charitable act. It's your Ten-Fold Marketing campaign, and that is a systemic strategy. The more your people embrace the idea, the more strongly they believe in the concept, the greater impact they will personally have in its success. So ask your team for their suggestions, or present a number of options and let them vote on it. Getting the team members involved from the start will help ensure their buy-in and their commitment to the success of the campaign.

There are so many worthwhile causes to choose from, you may be overwhelmed by the task of choosing just one. But there are a few factors to consider that may help you narrow down your choices. I suggest you begin by identifying a "short list" of charities or causes that appeal to you and your team on a personal level, then consider the following factors to determine which one is the best choice for your Ten-Fold Marketing campaign.

How efficient is the charity?

Charities that are registered as 501(c)(3) organizations are required to publish their financial statements, so it's possible to determine how much of their revenues are actually spent on their intended purpose. A website called Charity Navigator (www.charitynavigator.org) hosts a database of charities and rates each one as to how well they spend the monies they receive from donations. Charities that spend a large percentage of their funds on administration and advertising will be ranked lower than those who keep those costs proportionally low. It's not unusual to find non-profit organizations that regularly spend less than half of their money providing the services they were meant to provide. Looking for a charity that is efficient in the use of their funding may help you narrow your search for a cause that you and your business can embrace, so examine the efficiency of the organizations on your short list, and see if some can be eliminated based on that factor.

How marketable is the cause within your own market?

Think about who your company markets to, and consider which of the charities on your short list will be most popular with your customer base. If your target market is a local market, for example, you might want to choose a local non-profit organization to support. But if you are targeting a wider audience, focusing your Ten-Fold Marketing campaign on a local charity might not have the impact you hope for. Consider the demographics of your target market, and think about how your preferred clients will react to your supporting the causes you've identified on your short list. For example, imagine a company that sells fishing gear, that has a target market of fishermen between the ages of 35 and 65. Those fishermen might not be impressed to know that you donated $1000 to the March of Dimes, even though that is a terrific charity doing great things to help prevent birth defects. In that situation, the company might have a more effective campaign if they chose to donate that money to a fish and wildlife preserve or Ducks Unlimited.

How closely is the cause related to your industry?

A charity or a cause that is specifically related to your industry can be especially useful to a Ten-Fold Marketing campaign, for a number of reasons. First, as I explained above, your target market might already be aligned to the same cause. That is, the people who purchase your products and services will be those who also value a cause or charity related to those products and services.

Second, your customers will remember a related charity more readily than one that isn't related. And when they think of that charity, they will more likely remember your company as one that supports that worthy cause. An example of this would be a roofing company that supports Habitat for Humanity. There is a logical connection between the two, and a mention of one could prompt a potential customer to remember the other. When you can bring that kind of branding to your charitable giving, you'll be well on your way to a successful Ten-Fold Marketing campaign.

What feels right?

In the final analysis, the cause you choose to support should be the one that feels right. You'll be sacrificing your time, your money, your services, and your energies, and that will be easier and more rewarding if it's done for a cause that you truly believe in. If you have a true and personal connection with the American Cancer Society, or the local Cub Scouts, that connection can be your most powerful marketing hook of all. If you can tell your story, the "Why I Care About This Cause", you can bring your team and your customers to care about it too. And when they care, they'll gain respect and admiration for you, your company and your brand. That's the basis of Ten-Fold Marketing, and it can be a powerful component in growing your business. And more importantly, it's the basis for human compassion and a necessary step in growing your heart.

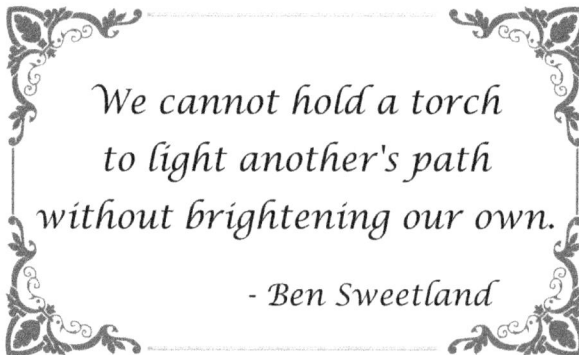

> We cannot hold a torch
> to light another's path
> without brightening our own.
>
> - Ben Sweetland

When you carry out
acts of kindness
you get a wonderful
feeling inside.

It is as though
something inside
our body responds
and says, yes,
this is how
I ought to feel.

- Harold Kushner

CHAPTER 8

Maximizing the Impact

Hopefully by now, your Ten-Fold Marketing plan is beginning to take shape, at least in your mind. As you move forward, from planning to implementation, you should think about how to maximize the impact of your efforts, not only for the people you help, but also for your business as well. When you commit to helping others, you naturally want to be sure your assistance is doing as much good as possible. Careful planning can assure that your money, your time, and your other assets will impact the people and organizations you have chosen to help. Additionally, your careful planning can help assure that you and your company get the best marketing bang for your efforts, so that you can reap those tenfold rewards we've been talking about. The key to success in this (or almost any business venture) is planning. So sharpen your pencil and let's get planning.

Impacting the Cause

Non-profit organizations, and the individuals they serve, seem to be in constant need. They need more money, more volunteers, more time, more influence, more, more, more. But let's face it, your ability to help them is limited. So you want to be certain that when you donate money, or time, or expertise or other finite assets to a cause, that your donations have the greatest possible impact on those organizations and individuals. There are a number of things you can do to help assure that, and it begins with choosing the right causes.

I mentioned in Chapter 6 that choosing the right cause includes identifying a group or individual where your impact would have its greatest possible impact. A small local charity might be impacted more by your donations than a large national one, but size alone shouldn't be your deciding factor. You'll also want to look into the organization's track record and see how much of their gross revenues actually go to providing services that make a difference. Very few non-profits can claim that 100% of their revenues are used to directly serve their constituents. That's because there will necessarily be administrative costs, marketing costs, insurance and other overhead costs associated with running a successful non-profit. So you should look for the ones who are able to keep those extraneous costs to a minimum, while funneling the majority of their revenues into the projects and the individuals for whose benefit the organization exists.

Non-profit organizations are all run by people. Corruption and incompetence exist in every industry, including charities. While most charities are run by honest, caring people who truly believe in helping their constituents, some are certainly more frugal than others, and a few will blatantly disregard their charters in exchange for personal gain. You owe it to yourself and your business to do some research to be certain that the group you choose to help will put your assistance to good and effective use.

The National Center for Charitable Statistics (NCCS)[5] maintains an online "Table Wizard" that gives you access to a broad set of national reports on nonprofits and charitable activities in the United States. You can customize the report filters to select from specific types of nonprofit organizations. Some of their services are limited to subscribers, but a basic search is openly available and is a great place to start your research.

According to the NCCS Table Wizard, there are currently over 1.5 million nonprofit organizations in the United States., so choosing the right one to partner with could take you some time. But I strongly urge you to do your homework, because if you choose poorly, your time and money could be wasted. As I explain in the next section, the public relations boost you were hoping for could turn into a public relations nightmare, should you align yourself too closely with the wrong organization.

Once you've decided which organizations or individuals you want to help, there are a number of ways you can maximize

---

[5] http://nccs.urban.org/

the impact your giving produces. One of the first steps will likely be to ask.

You should contact the organization directly, and let them know you are planning to make them one of your target charities this year. Most non-profits have an officer who acts as the Community Relations Coordinator, or Community Liaison, or Public Relations Officer. The title will vary, but someone in the organization will be the public face of the organization, and that person will be happy to take your call and answer your questions. Once you have that person on the phone, just ASK!

Tell them you want to help, tell them how much time, or money, or expertise you have to give, and ask them what you can do to maximize the impact of your giving. In small organizations, the Community Liaison might also be the Executive Director, in which case, he or she will know the answer to your question himself. But in larger organizations, he will probably have to refer you to someone else, and that's OK. You need to get to the person who knows the inner workings of the organization well enough to know how a donation of the size and nature you are considering will best be put to use.

You might speak to any number of individuals within the organization before you have a definitive answer. Be sure to keep all of their names and contact information, because as you'll see in the next section, they may be able to help you maximize the impact of your giving on your own organization as well.

Another great way to maximize your impact is to partner with other for-profit companies, and form a Ten-Fold Coalition of sorts. If you build a coalition of 5 companies, and each member agrees to donate $200 a month, you can then tell your non-profit that you'll be bringing them $1,000 a month. You'll be bringing greater benefit to the non-profit, and you'll have marketing partners that will all be working to maximize your Ten-Fold returns, along with their own.

Just before Christmas of 2011, Tory Johnson formed just such a coalition, though she may not have realized it at the time. Tory is the powerhouse behind the Spark & Hustle movement, CEO of Women for Hire, and regular contributor to both Good Morning America and Success Magazine, and in December 2011, she challenged her Spark & Hustle followers to spread some holiday cheer for families in need. "You may not know their names," Tory said, "but these are the mothers whose kids go to school with your children. They're the people who stand next to you in the grocery store. While we can't solve everyone's very real needs, this initiative is designed simply to bring a bit of holiday cheer to people who wouldn't experience that sunshine if it weren't for the kindness of strangers."

Tory set the goal for that holiday campaign at $1,000, and promised to cover the time and expense of administering it. She sent a video message out to her followers, and they responded with open hearts. Over the next 10 days, they raised well over $12,000 for those families, and at least some of those impoverished kids had a wonderful holiday, thanks to Tory Johnson and the Spark & Hustle community. Days later, when I saw the photos of those happy children with their new bikes and other gifts, my heart skipped a beat. As happy as those kids were, I can't imagine their joy was any greater than the joy those women felt for having made it all possible. The impact they'd had was so profound, and far greater than what any one of them could have achieved alone. But by pooling their resources and working together, they had accomplished something truly remarkable.

So, as you seek to maximize the impact of your Ten-Fold Marketing, consider joining forces with others whose goals align well with your own. Whether you are pooling money or talent or time or other resources, this kind of coalition can create a bigger impact – on the cause and on your business – than you can ever hope to create alone. And working with others on a project of that kind builds relationships and strategic partnerships that can have lasting benefits going forward.

Impacting Your Business

Now let's talk about how to get that Ten-Fold result from your charitable giving. Whether you're donating money, or providing volunteer hours, or working pro bono for the cause, Ten-Fold Marketing works best when you plan for maximum returns on your investment.

At this point, I can hear some of you raising objections. You may be thinking that charity is supposed to come from the heart, with absolutely no thought for your own personal gain. Well, if that's what you believe, then I certainly don't want to dissuade you from holding true to your beliefs. But my purpose in writing this book isn't simply to encourage you to do the right thing in terms of your soul. My purpose is also to help you grow your business. You can do that by unleashing the power of the social commitment that everyone embraces. When you do that, everybody wins. A rising tide lifts all boats.

If you are still unsure on this point, or if you believe that the concept of Ten-Fold Marketing is contrary to your faith, I suggest you look again at Chapter 1, under the sub-heading "Ten-Fold Marketing Isn't a Religious Dogma". But if you're ready to put this amazing strategy to work for your business (and your heart as well), let's get started!

> *Everyone has*
> *the power for greatness,*
> *not for fame, but greatness,*
> *because greatness*
> *is determined by service.*
>
> —*Martin Luther King Jr.*

Ten-Fold Marketing is like any other marketing in one important aspect. It only works if it AIMs at your specific target market.

Attract
Impress
Motivate

Your Ten-Fold Marketing strategy must attract, impress and motivate the people who are your very best prospects – your target market – or it won't do your business any good. So as you plan your strategy, be sure you consider the following components and incorporate them into your plan.

Attract Your Target Customers

In order for your marketing plan to work, it has to attract customers – to your website, to your opt-in list, or to door. And the first step in that process is to be sure they know about it. This is where Ten-Fold Marketing parts company with the idea that giving should be anonymous. Ten-Fold Marketing relies upon a very public gesture, and therefore you absolutely must make it known to the world – or at least to your target customers. You need to make sure that the customers you want to attract see you in the act of giving, so let's look at some ways to accomplish that.

Press Releases. A well-written, properly targeted press release can get your good deeds published in the newspaper or broadcast on TV or radio. We've all seen the pictures showing the President of ABC Company presenting a big check to XYZ Charity. Well, there's no reason you can't get your picture in the paper too, but you have to submit a proper press release to make it happen. A press release that is properly targeted and properly timed has a much better chance of being published than one that isn't those things. Submitting press releases to the wrong people, in the wrong format, at the wrong time will only waste your time and theirs. So, if you've never written a press release, or you've not had great success getting them published, I recommend you get some help with this. Shop around for a local PR firm, and ask for client references. And actually check those references. Don't just sign up with the first smiling face with the moniker, "PR" on their business card.

High quality photos will increase your chances of getting published in print media, and you can use those photos in your other marketing as well. A nice video can be used for your own website and YouTube channel, but it can also be compelling to reporters on both print and broadcast media, so make sure to capture some clips of you and your team in action.

Tell a story. Getting your story published is much more likely if you tell a compelling story. Tell about the people you're helping, and how their lives are impacted by your efforts. Think about the story about Tory Johnson and the hurricane aftermath. The details of Doris Banks's life, and the specific ways that Tory was able to help, make that story far more compelling than if the reporter had just said that Tory went to Texas to help people. Reporters are after those compelling stories, and if you give them a good one, you'll have a better chance at seeing it in print or on TV.

Newsletters. I can't think of any business that shouldn't be publishing a newsletter. Email programs like Constant Contact and MailChimp are so inexpensive and easy to use, I recommend them to all my clients as a way to stay in touch with all their contacts. If you have a newsletter, make sure you include articles, photos and videos about your Ten-Fold activities. Volunteering at the local library? Collecting toys for *Toys for Tots*? Donating canned goods to the Food Bank? Tell the story in your newsletter, and post it on your website or blog.

T-Shirts. Get your team t-shirts that announce your Ten-Fold campaign. These are great for branding too, and make good, inexpensive door prizes and giveaways for your networking events.

Networking. Many of you attend regular networking events as a way to meet and develop relationships with potential customers and referral sources. When you are out networking, tell folks that you're involved with XYZ Charity. Include it in your 30 second elevator speech. Get them interested in what you're doing. It will add new depth to your relationships and help you stand out from the crowd of networkers who are just trying to sell something. Never underestimate the power of a personal interaction.

Use the web. Use all of your Internet locations to get the word out about your Ten-Fold campaign. Post it prominently on Facebook, YouTube, Google+, Twitter, and any other Social Media sites that are frequented by your target audience. And *extend your generosity* to your chosen charities by giving them some free recognition and support on your pages as well.

Blog about the work you're doing with and for your chosen causes, and tell the stories that will compel your audience to see you in a favorable light. Tell the stories about how your chosen charity helps specific people with specific challenges.

Use everything you have. When people ask me, "How should I attract people to my website", I always say, "Any way you can!" So when it comes to attracting your target market, you should use every resource you have at your disposal. Be creative, and don't be shy. Tell the world (and especially your target customers) that you are generous, caring, and affiliated with a wonderful and worthy cause. That's how you attract people to your website, to your opt-in list, and to your door.

Impress Your Target Customers

The next step in your efforts to AIM for your target market is to *impress* them. As you work to develop your Ten-Fold strategies, you should keep in mind this important facet of your campaign. It has to impress the people who would be your very best customers. Who are they? What are their demographics? Are they mostly male, female, or do you serve both men and women equally? Are they beer and pretzels folks, or are they the champagne and caviar types? Do they have children at home, or are they already grandparents? How do they spend their free time? Are they liberal thinkers, or more conservative? Questions like these can help you develop a persona for your ideal customer, and that can help you target your energies toward impressing him – or her.

Hopefully, you've chosen your causes with your ideal customer in mind, so that, once they know of your generosity toward that cause, they will be instantly impressed. But how you present it in your marketing and public relations efforts can also play a role in impressing (or turning away) your potential customers. Remember to tell the story, as that will be the most compelling and most impressive way to let your customers know about your Ten-Fold activities.

Consider the difference between these two announcements.
1. ABC Company donated $1000 to the women's shelter last year, and the money helped house four families.

2. ABC Company saw a need in our community and donated the funds so that the women's shelter could provide safe emergency housing to four battered women and their eleven children last year. CEO Tony Jones said, "Getting these kids and moms out of an abusive situation and into a safe home is what matters most."

The additional detail is more compelling, and more impressive, because it begins to tell the story. So as you work to produce your Ten-Fold Marketing strategies, take the time to learn the stories that will help you impress the people you most need to impress – the people who will become your ideal customers, your target market.

Motivate Your Target Customers

The next step in your efforts to AIM for your target market is to *motivate* them to take action. Ideally, you'll motivate them to buy your product or service, but that may come later. Initially, you should work on motivating them to invite you in. Motivate them to visit your website, subscribe to your blog, Like your Facebook page or join your mailing list. Here are a few ideas I've seen work wonders as part of a Ten-Fold campaign.

1. Join our mailing list, and we'll donate a dollar to XYZ Charity in your name.
2. Help us reach 500 fans by June 1 and we'll donate $500 to XYZ Charity.

3. Like us on Facebook and learn how you can join our XYZ Charity team.
4. 10% of all orders this month go to XYZ Charity.
5. We support the XYZ Charity. Please help us by Liking our page.

Of course, once you have them on your website, blog, mailing list or fan page, that's when the real motivation has to take place. You have to use those other tools to build the relationships, trust, and motivation that will eventually lead to sales.

An important fact to remember about motivation is this:

> People *make* decisions based on emotion.
> They *justify* those decisions based on logic.

Get to know your customers so you can understand the emotions that will motivate them to buy. If you understand the emotions that motivate them, you can develop the Ten-Fold strategies that will trigger those emotions. Then make sure there's ample information available to them so they can logically justify their buying decision.

If you make a sale,
you can make a living.

If you make
an investment of time
and good service
in a customer,
you can make
a fortune.

- Jim Rohn

CHAPTER 9

Your Customer-Focused Strategy

In Chapter 3, I defined "*Marketing*" as *a systemic approach to increasing sales and enhancing a company's brand*, and I suggested you think about your marketing strategies in terms of your entire business, not just the marketing department. Later, in Chapter 7, I gave you my thoughts about identifying the focus of your Ten-Fold efforts – the causes, charities, and individuals that would be the recipients of your generosity, caring and philanthropy. In this chapter, I want to help you focus your efforts and your Ten-Fold thinking on the most important player in any marketing strategy – your customers.

In the American business community, there's a lot of talk about providing great customer service, but as a consumer, I've become aware that most companies aren't nearly as good at this as they claim to be – or as they think they are. So in this chapter, I am going to lead you through an assessment of your company's customer service, and talk about ways to improve upon the way you serve your customers, and they way you approach customer service.

So many companies focus their marketing efforts on finding new clients and cultivating new leads, but they completely ignore their *very best source of new revenue* – their existing clients! These are the people who already know you exist, already know you have products or services that they need, already know how to contact you, and have already purchased from you. These are the hottest leads going, and yet many marketing strategies never consider them as leads at all.

Tony Hsieh is the CEO of Zappos, the world's leading online shoe store, and he recognized the enormous value of marketing first and foremost to existing clientele. In his book, *Delivering Happiness*, he describes the strategy Zappos uses to keep their existing clients happy so they keep coming back. Hsieh understood that people can buy their shoes anywhere, but he wanted to assure that they always came back to Zappos first. So he led the Zappos team through a transition by which the core marketing strategy at Zappos would become their outstanding customer service. They moved most of their marketing budget out of "Marketing" and put it into hiring and training the very best Customer Service people on earth, and in so doing, moved Zappos from the brink of bankruptcy to the multi-billion dollar company it is today.

Hsieh writes, "Another common trap that many marketers fall into is focusing too much on trying to figure out how to generate a lot of buzz, when really they should be focused on building engagement and trust. I can tell you that my mom has zero buzz, but when she says something, I listen."

At Zappos, customer service is a priority for the entire company – not just the call center – and employees are judged not by how quickly they handle customer calls, but by how happy the customer is when they are through. They are committed – *really committed* – to giving every customer a delightful experience, so filling the order correctly is only a small part of serving the customer.

What I want to tell you about your Ten-Fold Marketing strategy is this: Grow your business by growing your heart, and start with the customers you already have. They will buy more, complain less, and recommend you to their friends when you have developed that engagement and trust. Spend your time and money on delighting those existing customers, and they will work better than any other marketing strategy you could ever employ for the same investment.

I am an American consumer, so I know that most companies that claim to deliver great customer service, actually deliver mediocre customer service at best. And one of the problems is that most people who work in "Customer Service" are the people with the least training, the lowest wages, and the least incentive and the least authority to improve the service they provide. If you want your people to provide great service, you have to empower them to serve. You have to teach them what great service looks like, and then give them the authority to make customers happy. At Zappos, that means call center employees have the authority to grant discounts on shipping, for example, without escalating a call to a supervisor. But even before giving them authority, you have to give them a sense of what great customer service really means within your organization. Many companies hire corporate trainers to teach a course on Customer Service to their employees, and, as a corporate trainer myself, I have recently added Customer Service to my own training portfolio. The following is an excerpt from that course.

A Primer in Customer Service

Let's begin by agreeing that "customer service" is not the goal. Your goal, if you hope to use this as a Ten-Fold Marketing strategy, has to go far beyond customer service – to the realm of utter customer delight. You have to do whatever it takes to turn a customer into an active and enthusiastic advocate for your products, your services, and your company. You want them fawning over your staff on Facebook, tweeting your praises on Twitter, chattering about you at church, and bragging on you at Bridge Club. And making that happen isn't easy but it's the goal of Ten-Fold Marketing. So where do you begin?

It begins with empathy. You have to have empathy for your customers in order to recognize and anticipate their needs and their wishes. Empathy is a skill that can be taught, but it's best taught in early childhood, so if you have employees who aren't empathetic, I suggest you keep them away from your customers. Sure you can try to teach a callous person to care about people, but I'm guessing you have better ways to spend your time. Hire caring people to handle your customers, and spend your time giving them the skills and authority they need to excel.

Recognizing the Levels of Service

You know that there are different levels of customer service, and I want you to know what they are so you can focus on what level you currently provide, and try to take your service up a level or two. We've all experienced these levels, but maybe you've never given much thought to it as a scale that can be measured. That's what I want you to do from now on. Recognize what you are doing now, so you can improve it and expand it going forward.

BASIC

There's nothing special about basic service. You go into a restaurant. You order food. The server brings you food. You eat the food. You don't die of botulism. That's basic. That's the bare minimum. If you're existing at this level, your company is doomed. Seek help immediately.

EXPECTED

This is the level of service we *expect*. You go into a restaurant. You order food. The server brings you food. He gets your order right. If you ordered a hot meal, it's hot. You eat the food. It tastes OK. You don't die of botulism. That's what you expected. You have no reason to complain, but you're not going to rave about it to your friends either.

DESIRED

This is a step above what you expect. This is what you hope for. You go into a restaurant. They seat you at a great table, with no screaming children nearby. The server is really good. He's charming, witty, and really cute. You order food. He brings you food. He gets your order right. It tastes great, and you still don't die of botulism. This isn't what you expect, but it would be nice, right? It's what you hope for when you go into a restaurant. A great table, a great waiter, a great meal. That's what we hope for. That's what we desire.

SURPRISING

For this level, I want to share with you a true story that happened to me at a restaurant in Istanbul, Turkey. I think you'll agree it's a good example of surprisingly good service.

My husband and I walked into a restaurant and were seated at a small table near the center of the room. The waiter asked what I would like to drink. I had been warned about drinking the water, so I asked him, "Do you have Diet Coke?" He said yes, and then asked for my husband's drink preference. Don ordered whatever he wanted, and then the waiter left the building. We watched him walk down the street and out of sight. He returned a few minutes later, carrying three cans of Diet Coke.

I had asked for Diet Coke, and rather than disappoint a paying customer, he went shopping for Diet Coke. That wasn't expected, or even hoped for. I never dreamed he would do that, so I didn't know to desire it. That was *surprising*! And that's the kind of service that gets people talking. I was surprised, of course, and delighted. And I have told my friends about that place. Now I've even written about it in a book. That's the kind of service that Seth Godin calls "Remarkable", because it is worthy of being remarked about. And that's the kind of service that can help you realize your Ten-Fold Marketing goals. But there's another level of customer service that, although rare, can pay huge dividends when the occasion presents itself.

UNBELIEVABLE!!

I have another story of truly amazing customer service, and this one also takes place in Istanbul, Turkey. My husband had been working in Turkey for some time, and my daughter and I had flown there to visit him. For days, Don had been telling us about his favorite Turkish dessert, a dish called Künefe. We had hoped to sample it while we were in Istanbul, but none of the restaurants we had visited had shown it on their menus. Now it was our last night in Turkey, and Don was determined to find us some Künefe.

As we walked down the streets of the city, we were approached by a number of "barkers", as I call them, young men whose job it is to coax and entice tourists to come into their restaurants for a meal. As each barker approached us, we'd look at his menu and then move on to the next, still hoping to find a place that offered Künefe. Looking at one menu, and not finding what we were after, Don looked at me and said, "They don't have it," and we started to leave.

The barker pleaded with us, "Yes, we have it! What is it?" And Don told the barker what we were looking for.

"Yes, we have Künefe," he said. "Chef knows Künefe."

Don replied, "No, it's not on the menu."

But the barker insisted. "Chef knows Künefe! Chef makes Künefe for you. We have it. Yes." And he practically dragged us to a table near the front.

Once we were seated, the barker had a brief conversation with our waiter, and then he left the building and went shopping. He returned a few minutes later with a bag of groceries, and indicated to us as he passed that it was the ingredients for Künefe.

We enjoyed our meal – and especially our dessert – and we learned another lesson from the Turks about customer service. Every time I hear the words, "Will Pepsi be OK?" I cringe, and I remember the way the Turkish businesses cater to their customers. As you work to create your own Ten-Fold customer service strategy, think about that, and challenge yourself and your people to reach for that *unbelievable* level of service, because that's the stuff that comes back to you tenfold!

Lest you think that exemplary customer service can't happen in this country, remember Zappos and ZocDoc and the countless companies – large and small – who push the envelope everyday. I have another example of truly surprising service that I witnessed right here in the United States.

I had a doctor's appointment at 2:15 one afternoon, and arrived, as instructed about 2:00. It was a pretty ordinary appointment, with a weigh-in and a check of my vital signs by the nurse, then a few minutes of waiting in the exam room, followed by a few minutes with my doctor. By the time I was ready to leave, it was almost 3:00 and it was pouring down rain outside. It hadn't been raining when I arrived, so I had left my umbrella in the car, but now the skies had opened up, and I was about to get drenched. I stopped by the reception window and made my follow-up appointment with the lady at the counter, and then she asked me to wait a moment before leaving. Soon, she came out from behind the counter, carrying a large umbrella. "Come on," she said, and she walked me out to my car, sharing the umbrella all the way. Once I was safe – and dry – inside my car, she headed back to the building.

That wasn't what I expected. I hadn't even thought to wish for it. I later learned that they keep a couple of big umbrellas in the office for exactly that purpose. They had anticipated my needs and had planned for the occasion that would eventually arise, when they could blow me away with their *surprising* level of customer service. It seemed unusual and unexpected to me, but to them, it was just another rainy day when they'd be walking patients out to their cars.

So think about how you can prepare for those scenarios in your own business. How can you anticipate your customers' needs and wishes? How can you capitalize on those events that might otherwise be seen as a negative experience for them? What can you do today and everyday to build the engagement and trust that creates customer loyalty? And how can you empower every employee to totally delight your customers with over-the-top customer care?

Never forget that every customer you have is also a potential customer. And they are the very hottest leads in your pipeline every single day. Treating them well, doing something good for them, being generous and caring and kind to them, will come back to you tenfold. I truly believe that, and I'm not alone. That's the Ten-Fold Marketing philosophy, and the core marketing strategy for some of the world's most successful companies. In the next chapter, I share the stories of several of those companies, small businesses from all over the country, who have embraced the Ten-Fold Marketing concept and put it to work, successfully, in their own businesses. I hope you'll find their stories as inspiring, motivating and uplifting as I have.

Part Four

Ten-Fold Successes

*No man who continues
to add something
to the material,
intellectual and moral
well-being of the place
in which he lives
is left long
without proper reward.*

- Booker T. Washington

CHAPTER 10

Ten-Fold Success Stories

Many of the stories I've related in this book have been uplifting and inspiring stories of hugely successful companies and people who have put the Ten-Fold Marketing concepts to work in their own lives. They may not have called it that, but they have lived lives that exemplify the generous, caring, and selfless behaviors that are the cornerstone of any Ten-Fold Marketing strategy. They have become household names like Oprah Winfrey, Zappos, and Ben & Jerry's, by being generous. They have grown their businesses by growing their hearts, and by giving people so much more than they expected that they have talked about it. Zappos customers and Oprah followers have spread the news of their generosity around the world, tweeting and posting and emailing and chatting about the awesomeness of the companies and the leaders they admire, and those companies and leaders have enjoyed massive success.

Now, in this chapter, I want to share with you the stories of Ten-Fold successes that have been realized by everyday people like you and me. Over the course of my research, I've heard dozens of stories from business leaders all across America, and these stories that have truly inspired me. I am in awe of the power of positive thinking and the generosity of everyday people that I have been blessed to meet as a result of this book project. Their kindness, generosity and selfless service have inspired me, and I hope they will inspire you as well, to develop your own Ten-Fold business model. These are business leaders, just like you, who have made a difference in their communities and their businesses by opening their hearts to help someone else. And each of them has realized rewards much greater than their investment in either time or money.

I have been impressed by these people and by their generosity, not only toward their chosen causes, but also toward me. They took time from their busy schedules to speak with me, tell me their stories, and respond to my questions. They were never promised anything in return, not even a mention in my book, and yet they invested their time – their most precious commodity – to help me. That alone is inspiring. And their stories are here to illustrate what a Ten-Fold Marketing strategy can look like, and how it can work in a variety of small businesses like yours. Some of these companies have seen remarkable growth in recent years, and the leaders I interviewed credit much of their success to the Ten-Fold concepts in leadership, mentoring, and marketing. Bryan Johnson is one such leader.

The Ten-Fold Story that Started it All

The inspiration for my book, *Ten-Fold Marketing: Growing Your Business by Growing Your Heart*, came to me first from my good friend, Kat Feder, in a speech she had given at one of our networking events. As she finished her remarks, she closed with these words about giving back to the community. "I truly believe," she said, "that whenever you do something good for someone else, it comes back to you tenfold." Of course, I had heard that sentiment uttered a hundred times before, and it didn't set off any buzzers when I heard it that day. But later that evening, a chance conversation with a couple of other friends started the wheels turning in my head. I want to tell you about that conversation because it just goes to show you that Kat was right, and the tenfold returns can come back to you from the most unexpected places.

I have worked, from time to time, as a web designer, and one of my favorite clients has been the New Beginnings Network Group. When I first met the group's organizers, Jeff Aames and John Tsaldaris (a.k.a. "JT"), an instant friendship was born – I liked them and they liked me, and I quickly became involved in their efforts to grow New Beginnings into a stronger, more diverse networking group. I agreed to build and maintain a website for the group in exchange for free advertising on the site. Any time they had changes to make to the website, Jeff would email them to me, and I'd get them posted on the site. It wasn't a big job, but paying a web designer for frequent updates would have been prohibitively expensive for the group. The fact that I would do it for free was really the difference between having a website and not having one, at the time.

On the evening after Kat had given her presentation (which happened to have been at New Beginnings), I was on the phone with Jeff and JT about some website updates.

Jeff: "Marianne, we are so grateful to you for doing the website for us!"

Me: "No worries, Jeff. I'm happy to help."

Jeff: "Well, we really appreciate it. We hope someday to be able to pay you for your services."

Me: "It's really no big deal. These edits will take me no time at all."

Jeff: "We're just so thankful to you for everything you do for us!"

Me: "Well, it's like Kat said today. Eventually it will all come back to me TENFOLD!"

And then I started laughing. I joked, "It's not about you guys. And it's not about me being nice. It's all about those TENFOLD RETURNS I'm going to get! It's all about ME! All this work is going to come back tenfold, and I'm going to be living large and rolling in the dough! Hell, this is my new marketing strategy!" We all had a good laugh about that, and went on to discuss the other topics on our agenda.

The next day, I completed the updates Jeff and JT had asked me to work on, and I sent them an email to let them know it was finished. And then, I remembered the phone call from the night before, and with a mischievous grin stretched across my face, I signed that email, "Yours in Tenfold Marketing, Marianne".

The minute I typed those words, I realized they were the title of my next book. Two years later, the book is finished, and it has spawned a whole new chapter in my life. I'm publishing an entire series of books about people in all walks of life who "Live Ten-Fold". I'm presenting workshops about how to "Grow your business by growing your heart". I'm leading a charge to involve more of corporate America in the Ten-Fold solutions to the world's biggest problems. And I'm loving life like never before!

None of that would ever have happened if I hadn't offered to build that free website. So I may not be living large or rolling in the dough, but my ROI on that website have been far greater than tenfold.

Bryan Johnson, Founder of Braintree, Inc.

One company that has fully incorporated the Ten-Fold concept into their corporate culture is Braintree, a company that provides credit card processing solutions to many of the most dynamic businesses in the world. I spoke with Braintree's Founder and Chairman, Bryan Johnson, about the Ten-Fold Marketing concept, and he shared some of his company's strategies for doing good in the world. "Among those strategies", he said, "is our Do Good Competition. We let the employees create Do Good Teams, and we give each team a certain amount of money. Their challenge is to maximize the good that they can accomplish with that money."

The Braintree culture has developed from its very beginning, with doing good as a core value, and that has become an integral part of the fabric of the company. In fact, the company's website (www.braintreepayments.com), includes what they call "The Braintree Compass":

The Braintree Compass

Be good, do good.

Help others succeed and celebrate their accomplishments.

Find reasons to be grateful and express it frequently.

Inspire others by being your best.

With this simple, selfless statement as their compass, Braintree has grown into a thriving leader in their industry. Founded in 2007, Braintree has achieved remarkable success in their industry. In 2011, they received a $34 million investment from Accel Ventures. Inc. Magazine named Braintree as the nation's 47th fastest-growing private company, with a three-year growth rate of over 4,000 percent. Johnson attributes much of their success to their adherence to that core value, "Be good, do good".

"A Little Kindness" Fosters a Chain of Giving

But Bryan Johnson's passion for doing good doesn't end there. He recently launched *alittlekindness.org*, a website founded on the idea of encouraging acts of kindness that can become part of a chain. As a visitor to the website, you'll be encourage to start a chain by performing some act of kindness. It doesn't have to be grand or expensive; it just needs to be something that will benefit another person. The recipient of that kindness is then encouraged to pass along a kindness to another individual. The idea is that each act of kindness encourages another, which in turn, encourages another, thus creating a chain of kindness. The next time you're feeling overwhelmed or discouraged, you should visit alittlekindness.org and start a chain. You'll be revived and uplifted in no time!

Ramona Rice, DeStress Express

Ramona is in the business of massage and skin care, and her company is frequently approached by charities and other non-profits and asked for gift certificates that they can give away. After all, who wouldn't love to win a door prize of free massage or facial? Ramona estimates that they give away about 10% of their annual revenue to charitable causes in the form of gift certificates.

Ramona's mom started the giving philosophy when she opened DeStress Express in 1996, and one of her first donations was four gift certificates to the local Jewish Community Center. It's interesting to note that the Jewish community in their town is only about 1% of the population, and many people might have thought it would be a waste of time to donate gift certificates to a charity with so few members in the community. The gift certificates were only valued at $25.00 each, the rate she personally charged for a massage at the time, but for the silent auction they raised over $400.00! The event organizers started to flood the spa with so many appointments they had to hire their first massage therapist and open another massage room in the tiny massage studio. That small community – just 1% of the town's population - now make up 10% of their business!

Fast forward to 2010, when DeStress Express expanded into a 3000 square foot spa with 10 massage rooms, a private natural nail suite, and advance skin care room. And every year they still donate to many causes, but particularly to those causes that 1% of the community support. Ramona told me, "Our motto with giving is that you never expect it to return back to you. You give because it is the right thing to do. When you give your time and talents to worthwhile causes, you show your community and potential customers your commitment and value. That is more valuable than any marketing plan."

Skye Callan, a Real Ten-Fold Leader

Skye Callan is Marketing Director at CKR Interactive, where she manages a team of employees and puts the Ten-Fold Leadership lessons to work every day. She gives special recognition to every employee and takes the time each year to make their birthdays extra special. She stays late the night before, and decorates their offices, so when they come in to work, the place is fun and festive, and they know she spent her own time and money to make it special. Skye says she likes to use kiddie themes (like cowboys, or dinosaurs, or pirates, or princesses), that match the employees personality or have some meaning in their lives.

A birthday is a very personal thing, and Skye goes out of her way to make it special for her team members. But that's just one example of the way she views her job. Being generous and caring with your employees builds team loyalty and camaraderie. And people naturally work harder, complain less, and go the extra mile for a boss they like and respect. Knowing you care about them is the first step in building that respect.

When she worked at LPS Solutions, Skye gave up her own raise and asked her boss to divide the money into bonuses for her employees. The department held contests and the winners took home the extra cash. She said that seeing their enthusiasm and joy was her Ten-Fold repayment. Skye Callan is definitely a Ten-Fold leader who has grown in her professional life by growing her heart.

Coach Jenn Lee

While I was gathering my research for this book, I happened to have a phone conversation with my friend and mentor, Jennifer Lee, whom I know has been living the Ten-Fold concept her entire life. I asked her if she could relate a story from her own experience that exemplifies the concept, and she hesitated.

"It's not about doing something good once, and getting a tenfold return," she said. "To me, it's about doing what's right all the time." Of course, I completely agree. But when I pressed her for an example, she told me about a day when she got an unexpected phone call from Jewish Family Services.

It seems that Jenn had stopped in at a local pottery studio in her area, and before leaving, had asked permission to leave a few brochures at their counter. Several days later, Marni Chepenik from Jewish Family Services has stopped by the pottery studio and had picked up one of Jenn's brochures. Eventually, Marni called Jenn to see if she might be willing to speak at one of their monthly meetings. "We can't pay you, but if you'd be interested, we would love to have you speak to our group."

Jewish Family Services is a non-profit agency whose goal is "to embody the time-honored tradition of community. . . of people helping and caring for one another." They offer services and programs that span across all stages of our lives. From one generation to the next, JFS's obligation is to feed the hungry, guide those in trouble and improve lives."[6] Jenn was impressed by their commitment to helping others, so she agreed to speak at their meeting without compensation.

Sometime later, Jenn was contacted by the Jewish Community Center of Greater Orlando, and honored to be asked to speak at their Mother Daughter Tea, an annual event that focuses on Women Role Models for young girls. Not only did they pay Jenn for that speaking engagement, but she felt truly honored to be included in the event.

"I'm certain that it wouldn't have happened if I hadn't volunteered to speak at the JFS meeting," she said, "but I don't believe that success comes about because of a single good deed. I believe that people do business with people they know, like and trust.   And people like and trust people that they know to be kind and generous - the kind of person who does the right thing every day, in ordinary situations."

She's right, of course. Ten-Fold Marketing isn't about doing a good deed and getting paid back in spades. It's about "Living Ten-Fold", and reaping the benefits that inevitably come from doing what's right.

---

[6] http://jfsorlando.org/

Jenn had another example that had just happened that morning. It was late in December, and Jenn was on the set at Fox 35 to do a segment about New Years Resolutions. In the "Green Room", she met some ladies from The Hair Cuttery, who were there to do a segment about celebrity hairstyles.

One of the hairstylists commented, "You must be the Life Coach they were talking about. You can just tell by your demeanor." They chatted briefly, and one of the stylist snapped some photos of her colleagues as the ladies were preparing for their segment. Jenn offered to take some pictures of them on the set.

"While I'm here, I could take some pictures of all of you," Jenn suggested. "You might like to post some photos on Facebook later." The ladies agreed, and thanked Jenn for doing them that favor. It was a very small favor, but it was genuinely appreciated, and that small act of kindness helped strengthen a bond that was beginning to grow between them. Eventually, one of the ladies suggested that maybe Jenn could come to speak at their regional conference of managers. It was a lead on a possible conference engagement that would probably never come up if Jenn hadn't offered to help them with their photos. That small act of kindness may one day reap some tenfold rewards. But Jenn has already reaped her reward for that kindness. She's living the life that she knows is right, and that is its own reward.

Tom Feeney, CEO of Safelite AutoGlass®

Tom Feeney has been instrumental in establishing Safelite AutoGlass® as a national company and a well-known brand in his tenure as President and CEO. Tom is a brilliant business leader with decades of experience, and he is completely committed to the company, its people and its customers.

Tom Feeney is also a man who has fully embraced the Ten-Fold Marketing concept, although he may have never called it that. He knows the value of providing over-the-top customer service and turning even a disappointed client into an advocate for his company. The Safelite blog includes a number of white papers on the topic of Customer Service, and it's apparent to anyone reading them that these are not just a company giving lip service to the idea of Customer Service. If you take a look at these documents (http://blogsafelite.com/index.php/site/strategies), I think you'll agree that these are the result of serious commitment and strategic planning designed to genuinely enhance the customer's experience. Tom Feeney recognizes that in his business (as in almost every business), a delighted customer can be a powerful marketing partner, and he has put his considerable influence into promoting great customer service from the ground up and from the top down.

But Tom is also committed to giving back to the community. He is the chairman emeritus for the American Red Cross of Greater Columbus Chapter, and currently serves as president of the Board of Directors for Ronald McDonald House Charities of Central Ohio. Tom is a board member for Champions of the Community Inc., a non-profit organization that manages the annual Nationwide Children's Hospital Invitational golf tournament. And he serves on a number of other boards for both non-profit and for-profit organizations throughout his community.

In September of 2011, the Safelite AutoGlass® Foundation hosted its first annual Charity Golf Classic, which welcomed approximately 160 representatives from suppliers and business partners from across the country, with fundraising efforts totaling more than $450,000 to be donated to the many charitable organizations the Foundation supports nationwide.

During the event, Tom Feeney encouraged guests to seek out ways to support their local communities as well. And this is where the Ten-Fold strategy really gathers steam. As a result of Feeney's appeal, several incredible stories of Ten-Fold Marketing have come forward.

John King, Vice President of Sika, Safelite's provider of urethane shared the following: "Having been inspired by [Tom Feeney's] "Challenge" to all present at Safelite's Inaugural Charities Foundation Golf Outing, we came back to Detroit, convinced that a lot of small things, add up in the end. So, the month of October, in our Sika Madison Heights, Industry Division Headquarters, we kicked off our First Annual Sika Coat and Clothing Drive for the needy of Metro Detroit. As a result, we took several full boxes of warm winter coats and clothing to the Salvation Army HQ's here, and we are feeling better as a result. Thanks for the inspiration, and we will let you know what other charitable initiatives we will become involved in going forward."

Mr. King later said, "The charitable involvement of the entire group of employees, at our Madison Heights, MI, facility, gave a sense that Sika cares about giving to others as much as our employees do. Giving gave all of us a double reward: benefitting those in need, and affirming Sika and its employees pride of doing something good for others."

Meanwhile, Doug Parnell, formerly the AGC Glass Company North America General Manager, was inspired to share his group's recent giving-back initiatives based upon his experience at the Safelite AutoGlass® Charity Classic. He said, "I have permitted our associates to take one paid day off per year to volunteer at some function or activity in the community. This year, three AGC associates (our controller, accountant, and CSR) did just that (note that we have a small office). They volunteered at the Children's Hunger Alliance Menu of Hope Luncheon. This event is one of the biggest fundraisers for this charity. Children's Hunger Alliance, established in 1970, is a statewide non-profit agency working toward long-term solutions to fighting childhood hunger. Their programs and services touch every county in Ohio, helping feed thousands of children each year."

When asked about how this philanthropy has helped his business, Parnell replied, "Our objective was to give to our community by providing an opportunity to our associates to do that while being paid. If anything, the objective was the encouragement and perquisite to the AGC associates. They appreciated that."

Tom Feeney has led the charge in his company and has embraced the concepts that are the cornerstone of the Ten-Fold

Marketing philosophy. "It's an altruistic approach to share our success beyond our four walls. We believe in investing part of our profits into the betterment of mankind. It brings personal satisfaction and pride for us to be known as a generous company."

He adds, "Part of our philanthropic strategy is to light a spark in individuals and companies we affiliate with to do their part to help others less fortunate than us. We want to be an example and inspire other individuals and business leaders to do what's right, to give back and to get involved."

And how is that strategy working out? Very well, I'd say. In fact, Safelite has seen a 102 percent growth in business since Tom Feeney became president in 2008, and he attributes much of that success to being fully committed to the well-being of the company, its people, its customers, and the community at large. That's Ten-Fold Marketing, and Tom Feeney and Safelite AutoGlass® are proof that it works.

Mindy Black, Inner Beauty Skincare

As the owner of Inner Beauty Skincare, Mindy Black has fully embraced the Ten-Fold Marketing principles, through both outstanding service to her customers, and in selfless service to her community. In her industry, as in so many others, customers base their choices on trust and confidence, not just on price. Mindy understands what it takes to build that trust and confidence with her clients, and she takes that aspect of her business very seriously.

In fact, it's been her reputation for over-the-top customer care that has helped her grow the business from its modest beginnings to the thriving enterprise it is today. And it's that same reputation for customer service that Tory Johnson recognized when she featured Mindy in the May 2012 issue of Success Magazine. As she said in that article, "This is personal, which means relationships and trust will trump price."

Mindy is committed to doing more for her clients and doing it better than her competitors. From the personal consultations she does with every new client, to the hand-written thank-you cards she sends, and everything in between, Mindy puts customer service at the top of her priorities. It's not an add-on or an afterthought; customer service is the very core of her business, and as such, it's naturally built into everything she does.

Mindy Black knows that great customer service is hard work, but it's good for her business, so she invests considerable time and effort in providing that superior level of service. It pays off in customer loyalty, customer referrals, and once in a while, in exciting and unexpected ways, like being featured in Success Magazine. But if you ask her why she does all this, she'll tell you it's because it's the right thing to do. "Inner Beauty Skincare was developed to empower other women to love themselves," she explains. "With that as my mission, I do everything I can to help make my customers feel important, empowered, and special. Because they are!"

But Mindy takes that commitment well beyond service to her customers. She extends her passion for empowering women to the young girls in her community that most feel the need for empowerment. In 2011, she founded "The Feisty Girl", an organization dedicated to helping young girls who may be the victims of bullying.

"This really means power and empowerment," she explains. "We want young girls to love themselves. We empower young girls to know that it is their inner beauty that is what is most important, and that it is ok to stand up for yourself, stand tall, shoulders back- put on your big girl panties and own it!"

Through The Feisty Girl program, Mindy works with the girls' inner confidence which exudes an outer glow. They host forums where the girls and their moms come together to discuss inner beauty, inner voices, insecurities, and even share stories of bullying.

"You see," Mindy shared, "I was the kid that was bullied for being Jewish when I was a younger, and then again as an adult. I lived in fear, I was insecure, I was afraid to stand up for myself, and I was afraid to love me. I didn't know what confidence was. I understand the pain associated with bullying and negativity. So now, it is my desire to help young women LOVE them for them."

Now she invites the girls to share their stories and to release the pain and fears associated with negativity and anxiety. They then talk about beauty and share skincare secrets where the girls and moms actually learn skin care first hand, and perform treatments on themselves. This promotes taking care of your self, face time with the mirror, and bonding with mom.

As a result of following her passion, and providing this selfless service to the women and young girls in her community, Mindy has been featured on the local news for "The Feisty Girl" and for Inner Beauty Skincare, two organizations that she has founded to empower women to love themselves.

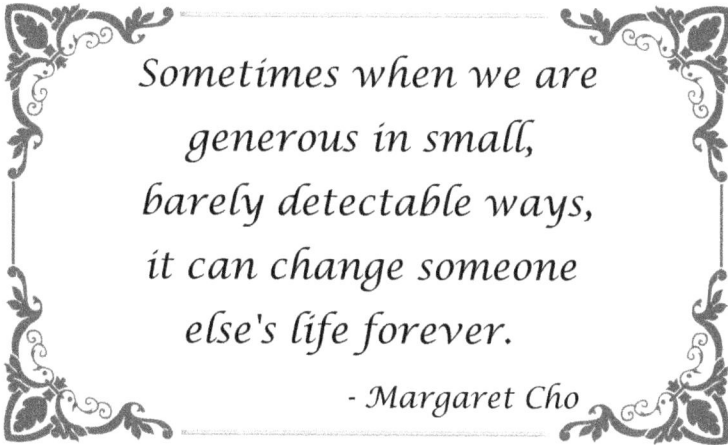

> *Sometimes when we are generous in small, barely detectable ways, it can change someone else's life forever.*
>
> *- Margaret Cho*

Jo Mousselli, Xtreme Lashes

Jo Mousselli knows more than a little bit about selfless service, and about the struggles a woman faces in daily life. As a wife and mother of four, she worked as an RN in a Pediatric Intensive Care Unit. Working with critically ill children and their moms, Jo used her compassion and caring, along with her medical training, to support the people under her care. Balancing her active family with a demanding career was always a challenge, and one she took great pride in doing very well. But in 2005, Jo was ready for a different challenge, and she wanted to begin a new career that would have a positive impact on everyday women like herself.

Jo knew first-hand the stress and pressures that women are under, and she recognized that there's a direct relationship between feeling good and looking good. So she put her experience, education, and passion to work and founded a new company in the beauty industry called Xtreme Lashes. She certainly didn't imagine back in 2005 that just a few years later her company would be the worldwide industry leader and the most respected name in eyelash extensions. But today, Xtreme Lashes is just that, and their products are available in over 50 countries, through thousands of beauty industry professionals who have been trained by Xtreme Lashes trainers.

Jo credits their explosive growth to a firm commitment to their core values. It would have been easier to grow the business early on if Jo hadn't been so adamant about proper training and safety standards. But she knew the long-term health of her company was better served by adherence to very strict standards and a commitment to safety and quality control. So she sacrificed short-term profits for long-term health, and stayed true to her personal commitments to her customers, her employees, and the beauty professionals who sold and serviced her products. As she said, "If the product isn't safe, or it doesn't look beautiful, or they don't last, then there's no chance for the business to last. Besides, that's just who we are. We believe it's the right thing to do and the only way to run any business. A happy customer is our best marketing tool, and we have to be committed to that."

You may never know
what results come of your action,
but if you do nothing,
there will be no result.

- Mahatma Gandhi

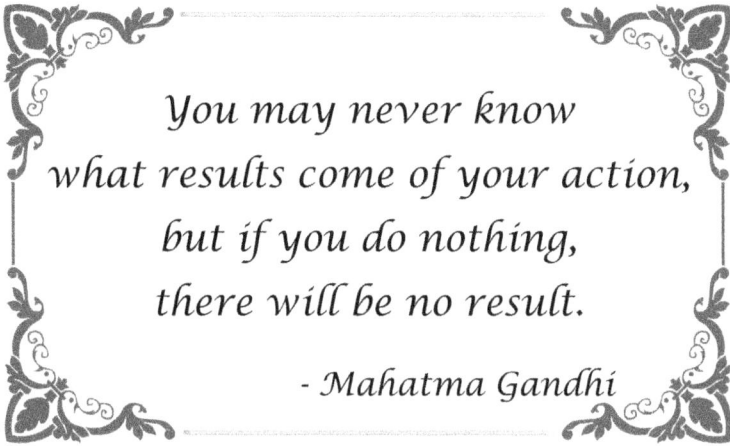

Misty Young, Squeeze In Restaurants

I absolutely love this story! And I absolutely love this company! And if I'm ever within 100 miles of one of their restaurants, I will absolutely go there! And apparently, I'm not alone. At a time when economic conditions are causing so many restaurants to close their doors, Squeeze In has opened two new locations, and adding another later this year. And they've done this, it seems to me, as a direct result of their Ten-Fold Marketing efforts.

I spoke with co-owner, Misty Young, about their community involvement, and I was amazed by the way they have embraced the idea of giving back to their community. Not only do they try to support *every single* non-profit who asks for their help, they openly seek more non-profits to help. The following excerpt from their website tells the tale:

We take great pleasure in donating to many worthy fundraisers, events, sponsorships and causes supporting schools, children, athletic programs, health promotion and more throughout the year. Our goal is to reach out to nearly every single group that requests our help and provide them assistance to reach their fundraising goals.

In addition to responding, we also proactively reach out, finding ways to serve our neighbors in Truckee and the Truckee Meadows. Our philosophy is that these are our communities too, and helping make them better helps us as well. It's just good business, it's the right thing for neighbors to help neighbors, and frankly, we just really love to be generous and giving.

Squeeze gift baskets are always a great silent auction item! Our gift baskets contain two custom Squeeze In coffee mugs, a bag of locally roasted gourmet coffee, a menu, a sticker, AND a $25 Squeeze In gift certificate good at any Squeeze In location.

Do you have an event or cause we could be involved in? Send us your request in writing. It doesn't have to be formal, just written. Please allow plenty of lead time for us to be able to accommodate your request.

Our address is:
10060 Donner Pass Road
Truckee, CA 96161

Hey! You can even do it right now while you're on the website! Just send your request to: info@squeezein.com

The website lists over 200 of the organizations and causes that Squeeze In has supported over the years, and they just keep looking for more people to help. Misty and her family have embraced the concepts that are germane to the Ten-Fold Marketing philosophy, and it's clearly working for them. The more they give, the more they get back, and not just in dollars, but in every way that matters.

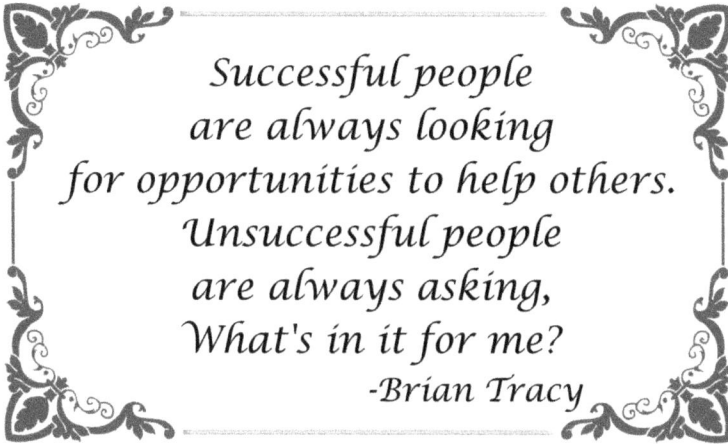

> *Successful people*
> *are always looking*
> *for opportunities to help others.*
> *Unsuccessful people*
> *are always asking,*
> *What's in it for me?*
> *-Brian Tracy*

Cassy Aoyagi, FormLA Landscaping

La Cañada Flintridge is a small town in Los Angeles County, California whose public library boasts very impressive botanical gardens, called "Gardens of the World". These gardens were designed to highlight planting options from the five regions of the world whose climates are compatible with that of California: California, of course, the Mediterranean basin, Australia, Chile, and South Africa.

Cassy Aoyagi's company, FormLA Landscaping, collaborated with La Cañada Valley Beautiful, a local non-profit dedicated to beautifying the community's open spaces. In partnership, they transformed the Library's gardens of ivy into a robust, diverse and beautiful example of water-wise landscaping as the recent drought approached. The goal was to show the huge variety of beautiful plants that could remain beautiful with limited water and no artificial fertilizers or chemicals. These are important goals anywhere, but especially in California. These measures could help protect the delicate water table, reduce Southern California's astronomical water importation costs, and protect the health and safety of children and pets that come in contact with the gardens.

When the project was first envisioned, Cassy offered her design and presentation time free of charge, as a way of educating the city and the public in light of the water resource challenges. It became a larger project over time, and she also had to educate the County and the City officials in order to secure the additional resources. Eventually, Cassy was inspired to find new ways to share her vision and educate the community.

The first garden approved was the largest space, the California Native gardens. It was also Cassy's largest investment of time, since the idea of an all-native garden was still largely misunderstood. Cassy focused on creating a garden and a program that would educate the public and serve as a demonstration garden for the eco-friendly landscaping she had envisioned. Once the garden was finished, Cassy provided personal tours to many folks who wanted to know more about the garden. She responded to some initial concerns about the small size of the plants. The garden was over 3000 square feet, and when it was first completed, it looked like a lot of mulch, with very little greenery. It was important to educate the community about long term planting for sustainability, plant health and reduced maintenance. On the heels of that initial education, people were asking to learn more, so Cassy organized multiple garden events, tours, and educational materials to help interested parties understand what the garden is, and why it is in place.

More recently, however, the non-profit that had been funding much of the work saw its funding diminished as a result of the harder economic times, and the garden's maintenance service was cut. After the cuts, Cassy created maintenance workshops that would bring more awareness to the garden, and also give visitors hands-on experience maintaining these types of gardens. As a result, the gardens are beautifully maintained, and the community is highly invested in them.

These maintenance days have turned into great networking and client development opportunities. Cassy dedicates her own time and the time of her team leaders. Their interest in the community and the time they spend mentoring volunteers has resulted in industry speaking opportunities for Cassy and her staff. They receive invitations to participate in garden tours. It also won fans at the City, the Library and with the sponsoring non-profit, La Cañada Valley Beautiful, resulting in recommendations to homeowners and businesses in the area.

Throughout the years that they've provided personal tours, public events and now workshops, the interest in the garden continues to grow. Cassy's clients are aware that she was the mastermind behind their unique demonstration garden at their local library. In recent years, more and more potential customers call her for sustainable landscaping services. The library accomplishments provide FormLA Landscaping with more credibility as they put their money where their mouths are. They are more than just a service provider. It shows that they care about how people develop their land and they want to find ways to help them do it right.

If Cassy had simply done good work and been paid for it, most of the community would still be unaware of her talents. Today, FormLA Landscaping is a high-profile, custom sustainable landscape firm which services celebrity clientele.

When I asked her about how her volunteerism has affected her bottom line, she said, "I feel as if I've accomplished something that is impacting on a community more than I could ever do in my normal business....I've made a difference and I know it. The benefits are numerous and you just can't place a monetary value on them."

Deborah Shane, Author, Speaker, Strategist

Deborah Shane learned about the power of kindness at an early age. Inspired and supported by a father who truly believed in her, Deborah has spent her life following the dreams he helped her envision, and helping others live the dreams they see for themselves. Today, Deborah is a career author, branding strategist, nationally published writer, speaker and media host.

"The power of kindness is bigger than just about any other thing we have to give," she says. "It has been for me and it has opened the path to so many amazing opportunities personally and professionally."

And opening paths is exactly what it has done for her! In recent years, Deborah has published her book, *Career-Transition-Make the Shift*, exploded her own blog and written for numerous other national websites and blogs. She has been featured in *SmallBizTrends.com*, *Careerealism*, *PersonalBrandingBlog.com*, *AmexOpen*, Monster, and *Blogher.com*. She has spoken at several national conventions such as Tory Johnson's *Spark and Hustle*, *Blogher*, and *XPO NY*. Her business tips have been included in Tory Johnson's new Spark and Hustle book, and new book by MSNBC host of *Your Business*, JJ Ramberg. She's been featured on two national tele-calls for Tory Johnson's *Virtual Job Club*. She has hosted over 240+ guests, including media anchors, authors, entrepreneurs and journalists on her own BlogTalk Radio Business Show, now in its 3rd year, and has close to 41,000+ downloads!

Deborah is certainly enjoying the fruits of her labors, but she says it all comes back to the core values she learned from her parents. "I grew up seeing my parents give, help and share. It always made sense to me, and was something I felt good that they did because I saw how it affected others." Today, she takes great pleasure in helping others develop the plans that lead them to their own dreams and successes. It's not so much a strategy for business, as it is a strategy for living. But business is part of that, and a caring attitude benefits your whole life, including your business. So Deborah is thankful for her parents' teachings, and tries always to follow their example, leading with kindness, generosity and an attitude of paying it forward.

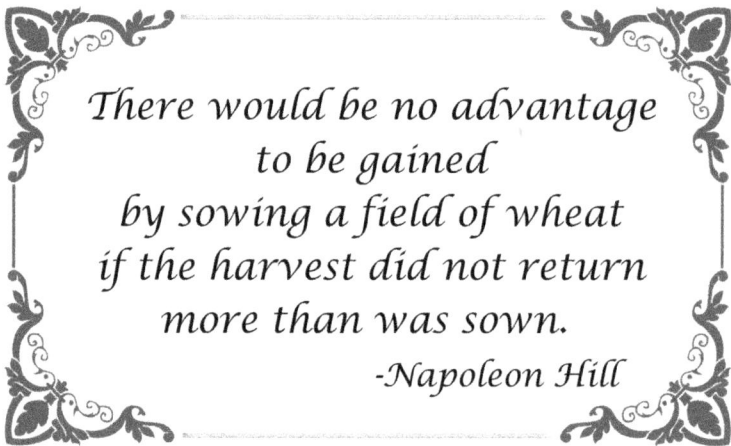

> *There would be no advantage*
> *to be gained*
> *by sowing a field of wheat*
> *if the harvest did not return*
> *more than was sown.*
> *-Napoleon Hill*

David Rust, Good Guys Group

Two years ago David Rust and Shane Moore formed a networking group called the Good Guys Group or G3. Their sole goal was to "Pay it Forward" to other members and the community at large. In the course of recruiting business leaders for their group, they met a gentleman named Brad Closson who came to know them as good people, and as the principals in their wealth management practice.

Because David and Shane help people who have come into wealth through retirement, divorce, inheritance, lottery, etc., Brad convinced them to write a book. He helped them find a publisher and he continues to assist them with promoting the book and their company.

It's been quite a journey for David and Shane. Their book, *Sudden Wealth...It Happens*, was released in September of 2011 and the positive changes to their world, both personally and professionally, have been profound.

Their own positive experiences most recently revolve around the many activities that surround them now as new authors. They have been asked to speak to Universities, business clubs, women's book clubs, and a bottled water national distributor chain. Their belief that Sudden Wealth carries many psychological challenges along with the financial ones, has created partnerships with a few well established psychologists in Austin. These psychologists have agreed to help them deliver these important messages in speaking engagements and with their own clients. Now they are planning to launch a second book with these same psychologists! Prospective clients are regularly seeking them out, and referrals are coming in at a rapid pace!

"We are floored with the response from our book, and very grateful to Brad for starting us on our journey. We can't thank him enough", says Rust. "From his selfless act of making a recommendation to us, and then staying on us until we acted."

And all of this came about because David and Shane wanted to do something good in their community. "It's all because someone got involved and Paid it Forward."

Deb Haupt, Haupt Antiek Market

Deb Haupt owns an antique store in Apple Valley, Minnesota, and she has a terrific story of Ten-Fold Marketing success in her business. I just love this one.

A few years ago, a woman from New York was in Apple Valley on business, and stopped in Deb's shop. The woman had expected to fly on to France that day, but because of the "Shoe Bomber" incident, her flight was delayed, so she had extra time on her hands. After a stroll through Deb's shop, she asked Deb if she knew of any other fun antique and vintage shops where she could spend her new found time. Deb loves to recommend other local small businesses, so she gave the woman a list with directions and enough fun places to fill her day.

A few months later, Deb was leading a tour group to Provence, in the south of France, to shop the flea markets. Guiding tours is a side job related to owning an antique market – and one that she really enjoys. Deb wanted to make sure that the information that she was receiving over the internet was accurate, so she sent an email to a woman that has a blog about shopping the brocantes (the flea markets) and living in France.

Deb explained that she was bringing a tour group and wanted to verify some information about the region, and the blogger recommended she speak to her friend Mimi. It seems that Mimi is also an American, living in Provence, and she was about to marry a Frenchman. So Deb and Mimi emailed each other, and Mimi told Deb she'd be back in America in a few days and would call her on the phone.

"The first words out of her mouth were amazing to me," Deb said. "Mimi said to me, 'Deb, we have met before, I came into your shop a few years ago and you set me up for this wonderful day of shopping in Minnesota.'"

Deb admits now that she didn't remember Mimi from that brief encounter. "I recommend other shops all the time, so what I did that day a few years ago didn't stand out to me. But now she was in a position to help me back!"

Mimi recommended changes in Deb's itinerary in France and told her about the small town Provencal markets. She even joined the tour group for two mornings while they were in France, and helped negotiate their flea market prices. She gave Deb and her group the inside scoop. She and some friends opened up a small brocante (sale) in her home and invited the group to shop at her old French country home. They had wine and French cheese and crackers. It was an amazing, unexpected experience, and one the entire group will remember with fondness.

When I asked Deb about the whole experience, she said to me, "I believe that kindness always comes back to you. Sometimes in ways you never imagine."

Cathy Alinovi, Country Vet

I first met Cathy Alinovi at a Tory Johnson event, and we initially became friends because of two things we have in common: We both love dogs, and we are both from small towns in Indiana. When I asked Cathy if she had a story of Ten-Fold success, she hesitated at first, and then related the following story to me, that I believe speaks to the core of the Ten-Fold philosophy.

"This woman lives about two hours from me and has two seizure dogs – crazy seizures – like bloodcurdling scream, paddling on the floor, back arched, poop and pee all over themselves - horrible seizures. She originally had one seizure dog, but figured she could handle anything, so she adopted another one from a family who was probably going to have this young boy euthanized. She's a really neat woman. A retired researcher from a Midwest university, her family has either passed on or moved away, and she cares for these dogs better than anyone could. The anti-seizure medication almost killed one of her dogs, so she had to reach out to people who would look at things differently to help save her four-legged family. Somehow she found me about a year and a half ago.

"Two hours is a long way to drive, especially if one of the pups has a seizure on the way here. But she now comes every two weeks to take care of the kids. And she comes when she has emergencies – if she can't handle it at home through e-mails, texts

150

and talking on the phone. She is a retired PhD after all – but she never tells you that – she's not pushy about it; she just wants to take care of the kids. But boy is she smart! So over the course of a year and a half, we talk about things. And share things as friends would. She's fabulous with the computer – She helps me transfer files to my iPad, shows me tricks I didn't know, helpful things. And her appointments take a bit longer. I normally schedule 30 minutes for a repeat visit, but we schedule 2-3 hours for her and her kids. And we talk, and we take care of the four-legged children. A colleague of mine, who lives 35 minutes away, now offers to come to help take care of the pups, because this client and the amazing care she gives to her dogs inspire people to help. My whole staff feels this way too.

"In our sharing, she has told us about a friend she has known since she was a child. He is her soulmate – but he is from a very private Native American tribe and she cannot be his wife by their traditions. Thirty or 40 years later, they are the best of friends – They e-mail all the time (Computers are allowed.). He shares some of his herbal knowledge with her, and she passes along the information to me – information that has helped her dogs, and other patients of mine. I have been so appreciative of his help that I've wanted to return the favor. However, outsiders are not allowed and I don't think a batch of chocolate chip cookies really is fair trade!

"Now, he is carving a medicine wheel for me, just because – I didn't ask for one – He asked his friend to see if I would like one!! They are beautiful, and I am deeply honored. I really can't express how it makes me feel. In return, I continue to take care of all the four-legged brothers and sisters (as his custom calls them) that people bring to me, knowing I have friends I've never met over a thousand miles away.

"My answer to your question of what has come back to me Ten-Fold is just this: Relationships. I donate time and money to local 4-H and the grade school and a million little things with never a thought of what I get back. I do it because I want to, and I'm blessed to be in a position where I can. What I get back is relationships from people who have strong family values; I become part of that family - involved with their four-legged family members."

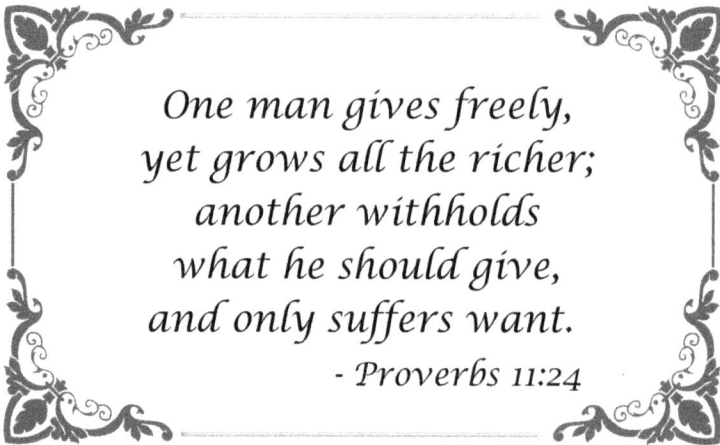

> *One man gives freely,*
> *yet grows all the richer;*
> *another withholds*
> *what he should give,*
> *and only suffers want.*
> *- Proverbs 11:24*

José Alejandro Flores, VOS®

VOS® is a company that manufactures and distributes natural rubber footwear, and they are a Ten-Fold company through and through! Their founder, José Alejando Flores, began the business with a commitment to a global social initiative that he calls Give+Give+Recycle™.

The company provides basic healthcare and education to the natural rubber producing communities which cultivate the sustainable raw material for the VOS® flips, initially in Guatemala. In addition, VOS® also provides shoes to individuals in need of footwear. They have already done shoe disbursements in the U.S. and various regions throughout Latin America.

As a result of these unselfish humanitarian gestures, the company has flourished and grown, and the brand is now recognized throughout the U.S. and beyond. But when I asked José about the Ten-Fold returns his initiatives have fostered, he said, "First and foremost is the pleasure which we are able to share with the recipients of our humanitarian work. It is amazing how these small but significant gestures can greatly change for the better the lives of individuals in need. The most important business benefit is that the humanitarian foundation reflects an organization that makes sound and just decisions both on an internal and external basis while treating its partners and staff with utmost respect."

Debbie Swanson, Abrasive Resource Inc.

When I was doing research for this book, I met Debbie Swanson, President of a company called Abrasive Resource that sells industrial quality sanding supplies. I didn't know a thing about this industry, and I assume you don't either, so before I tell you about their Ten-Fold Marketing story, let me tell you a bit about their industry.

Abrasive converters like Abrasive Resource buy great big rolls of abrasive cloth and paper in bulk—similar to the way fabric comes on great big bolts or rolls for clothing manufacturers. But, rather than make the fabric into shirts, Abrasive Resource converts the abrasive paper into sanding discs, abrasive belts and all sorts of other sanding supplies. Typically, converters have a very fast turn-around from manufacturing to shipping, which usually is a big asset to the manufacturers who are their customers, because they don't need to stock a lot of inventory in their manufacturing plants. Since they know that they'll receive their order in less than a week, they wait to reorder supplies until they open their last box of sandpaper. This could be a problem, however, if a convertor needed to shut down for some reason (moving their facility, upgrading equipment, etc.). Converters like Abrasive Resource would always want to give their customers plenty of notice if lead times were going to be longer for any reason.

The abrasive converting industry is a small one -Everyone pretty much knows their competitors personally or certainly by reputation! Back in 2005, the devastation of Hurricane Katrina hit one of Debbie's competitors in Louisiana and their business was shut down for about two weeks. Many of their manufacturing customers were affected, and the ripple effect a shortage of abrasive supplies could create for their manufacturing plants was a potential nightmare. The competitor's facility was just over a hundred miles away from New Orleans—far enough that they didn't sustain physical damage, but close enough that there wasn't any phone or internet service for days and even weeks in some areas. Their manufacturing facility was in fine shape—they just couldn't communicate with anyone! They couldn't call, fax or email out and no one could reach them either. Their customers needed supplies, and when they couldn't reach their usual supplier, began to panic. They turned to the Internet, which is—of course—the way Debbie became involved directly with their customers. It turns out that Abrasive Resource was one of the first abrasive companies on the Internet, and because they carried some of the same product lines, their website was appearing for all of the web searches these manufacturers were typing into Google in their attempt to find a replacement supplier quickly.

Debbie's staff quickly determined that they would accept all of their competitor's orders - on behalf of their company. They filled orders for five days before they were even able to reach the competitor, as phone lines, internet and cell phone service were all disabled there. Debbie told them of their decision, and then together, determined a plan for moving forward. Abrasive Resource would invoice their competitor at their cost, and allow them to invoice their own customers once they were back on their feet again. All of the profits for those orders would go to the company affected by the hurricane.

Debbie said, "It was an easy decision. We simply did what we hoped someone would do for us if we were in the same situation. We even went as far as putting a "do not sell" notation on these customer's profiles in the computer, so that if they later contacted us for a reorder, we could redirect them back to our competitor."

Now, fast forward a few years. That competitor was eventually bought out by a large supplier, and the new corporate suits made the decision to close down the abrasives converting facility in Louisiana. One by one, their customers contacted Abrasive Resource. They remembered the service that Debbie's team had provided back in 2005, and when they could no longer buy through the competitor, they called Abrasive Resource and became their new customers. They liked the way Abrasive Resource did business, and rewarded them years later by paying it forward and returning the favor to them. The Ten-Fold Marketing philosophy had proven itself once again.

*I expect to pass through
this world but once;
any good thing therefore
that I can do,
or any kindness
that I can show to
any fellow creature,
let me do it now;
let me not defer
or neglect it,
for I shall not pass
this way again.*

- Ettiene De Grellet

CHAPTER 11
Your Turn

Writing this book has been both enlightening and rewarding, and I hope you've found reading it to be equally so. I've been amazed and humbled by the outpouring of support from people all over the country – and beyond – who have shared with me their time, their talents, their stories, and their passions, with nothing expected in return. It has definitely been one of the feel-good experiences of my professional career, and I hope it has made you feel good too. But my goal in writing this book isn't about spreading euphoria and warm, fuzzy notions about doing good deeds in the world. My goal is to help you develop a marketing strategy for your business that can help you grow your bottom line. If you get to feel good doing it, that's an added bonus.

So take some inspiration from the stories I've told here, and follow the strategies I've laid out. Or develop your own, if you feel inclined to do so. But don't just put down the book and say, "Gee, that was nice." Ten-Fold Marketing can and does work for the companies that put it to use, and it can work for you. So I challenge you now to write your own Ten-Fold game plan.

Determine how you can use these principles to grow your own business, and then make it happen, starting today.

Identify your focus, identify your assets, and put them to work for your business. Maximize the impact through traditional and social media, and use your generosity and caring to attract, impress and motivate your target market.

If you need further inspiration or ideas for developing your own Ten-Fold strategies, visit my website at www.livetenfold.com. There, you can read about other Ten-Fold companies, and even post your own Ten-Fold success stories. I definitely want to hear from you as you work to grow your business by growing your heart.

You've seen these strategies work for companies large and small, in big cities and small towns, across a variety of industries and corporate structures. Ten-Fold Marketing can have a powerful impact on your employees, your customers, your community, and your business. Now it's time to put what you've learned into practice. Now it's your turn to live Ten-Fold!

Part Five

Other Stuff

About the Framed Quotes

The quotes that appear throughout the book were gathered from a variety of sources and are intended to provide inspiration and motivation, as well as evidence of the global acceptance of the concepts presented throughout the book. While you may be familiar with many of the quoted authors, others may not be familiar to you. So I've included these brief notes about each one and encourage you to further explore the writings and teachings of these very wise individuals. They are listed here in alphabetical order by last name. Some of the names were new to me as well, and I'm never really sure which name is the "last name" in some other cultures. So if I've messed that up, I apologize.

1. **Aesop** – (c. 620-564 BC) a Greek fabulist credited with having written a number of fables. You may have read some of *Aesop's Fables* yourself.

2. **Mary Ann Allison** - an interdisciplinary scholar at Hofstra University who uses media theory, sociology, and complex

systems theory to study the ways in which individuals, communities, and institutions are changing.

3. **Sri Sathya Sai Baba** - (1926 – 2011) an Indian guru, spiritual figure, mystic, philanthropist and educator.

4. **Henry Ward Beecher** - (1813 –1887) a prominent Congregationalist clergyman, social reformer, abolitionist, and speaker.

5. **H.S.M. Burns** – Past President of Shell Oil Co.

6. **Margaret Cho** - an American comedian, fashion designer, actress, author, and singer-songwriter. She has won awards for her humanitarian efforts on behalf of women, Asians, and the gay community.

7. **Sir Winston Churchill** - (1874 –1965) a British Conservative politician and statesman (twice elected Prime Minister), known for his leadership of the United Kingdom during World War II.

8. **Barbara De Angelis** - an American relationship consultant, lecturer and author, TV personality, relationship and personal growth adviser.

9. **Ettiene De Grellet** - (1773-1855) author and Quaker Missionary.

10. **Charles Sherlock Fillmore -** (1854 – 1948) founder of the Unity Church, he became known as an American mystic for his contributions to metaphysical interpretations of Biblical scriptures.

11. **Mahatma Gandhi** – (1869 – 1948) led India to independence and inspired movements for non-violence, civil rights and freedom across the world.

12. **King George VI** – 1895 – 1952) King of the United Kingdom from 1936 until his death in 1952. He was the last Emperor of India, and the first Head of the Commonwealth.

13. **Johann Wolfgang von Goethe** – (1749 –1832) considered the supreme genius of modern German literature.

14. **Whoopi Goldberg** - an American comedienne, actress, singer-songwriter, political activist, author and talk show host.

15. **Napoleon Hill** - (1883 – 1970) an American author, widely considered to be one of the great writers on success. His most famous work, *Think and Grow Rich* (1937), is one of the best-selling books of all time.

16. **Martin Luther King, Jr.** (1929 – 1968) civil rights leader and Nobel Peace Prize recipient.

17. **Harold Kushner -** a prominent American rabbi aligned with the progressive wing of Conservative Judaism, and a popular author.

18. **Henry Wadsworth Longfellow** (1807 – 1882) an American poet and educator.

19. **General of the Army Douglas MacArthur** (26 January 1880 – 5 April 1964) an American general and Chief of Staff of the United States Army during the 1930s. He played a prominent role in the Pacific theater during World War II, and received the Medal of Honor for his service.

20. **Rig Veda -** an ancient and sacred collection of Vedic Sanskrit hymns from India.

21. **Jim Rohn** - (1930 - 2009) an American entrepreneur, author and motivational speaker. His rags to riches story has influenced many others in the personal development industry.

22. **Arnold Schwarzenegger** - an Austrian and American, former professional bodybuilder, actor, businessman, investor, and politician.

23. **General Norman Schwarzkopf** - a retired United States Army general who was commander of the Coalition Forces in the Gulf War of 1991.

24. **W. Clement Stone** - (1902 – 2002) a businessman, philanthropist and New Thought self-help book author.

25. **Ben Sweetland** – American author, best known for his best-selling book *Grow Rich While You Sleep*.

26. **Rabindranath Tagore -** (1861-1941), author and poet from Bengal, he became the first non-European to win the Nobel Prize in Literature in 1913.

27. **Brian Tracy** – American business leader, self-help author and motivational speaker.

28. **William Arthur Ward** - (1921–1994) author of *Fountains of Faith*, Ward is one of America's most beloved inspirational writers.

29. **Oprah Winfrey** - an American media proprietor, talk show host, actress, producer and philanthropist. She is also,

according to some assessments, the most influential woman in the world.

30. **Larry Winget** - is a motivational speaker, author and television personality. Winget markets himself as the trademarked "Pitbull of Personal Development" and "World's Only Irritational Speaker".

31. **Zig Ziglar -** American author, salesman, and motivational speaker.

About the Author

Marianne Carlson graduated *Summa cum Laude* in 1997 from the University of Maryland (European Division) with a BS in Information Systems Management. Since then, she has managed a diverse career in Information Technology, Marketing, and Training.

She served as the Computer Support and Training Coordinator for the Vermont Judiciary, where she managed a team of 18 Power Users who led the Judiciary through the challenging transition from "dumb terminal" computing era into the world of personal computers. In 2000, the Power User team, under Marianne's leadership, was honored as a State of Vermont Outstanding Team for Public Service, the only team from the Judicial Branch to receive such an honor.

September 11, 2001 was a defining moment in her life. Although she had no close friends lost in the terrorist attacks that day, she was deeply moved by the patriotism that embraced the nation, and she felt a new and powerful sense of national pride and commitment. She vowed, "If my country ever needed me, I would be proud to serve." She could not have imagined on that day that such a call would ever come, but in November of that year, she and her husband Don moved with their two youngest children to Wiesbaden, Germany, and her life's greatest story began to unfold.

In 2003, shortly after the war began, Marianne served a six-month deployment with the US Army in Balad, Iraq. It was an experience that has defined her life and reshaped her motivations.

Over the course of her husband's career, Marianne has lived in five different countries, five different states, and countless cities. So when her husband retired, they chose central Florida as their permanent home, and started Emcie Media, a business that allows her to pursue her passions for marketing, writing, teaching and public speaking.

Additional Resources

The following pages include several web addresses that are listed here in order to extend the value of this book beyond what I've started here. It is my hope that you will find them valuable as you pursue your passions and begin your Ten-Fold journey. As your story progresses, I would love to hear from you. Please visit the Ten-Fold website and let me know how it's going.

www.livetenfold.com

My other websites:

www.mariannecarlson.com

www.emcie.com

www.bestinbusiness.us

www.facebook.com/emciemedia

Contributors' websites
(in the order in which they appear)

www.toryjohnson.com

www.sparkandhustle.com

www.womenforhire.com

www.zocdoc.com

www.newbeginningsnetworkgroup.com

www.braintreepayments.com

www.alittlekindness.org

www.destressexpress.com

www.ckrinteractive.com

www.coachjennlee.com

www.safelite.com

www.usa.sika.com

www.na.agc-flatglass.com

www.innerbeautysc.com

www.xtremelashes.com

www.squeezein.com

www.formlainc.com

www.deborahshane.com

www.g3austin.com

www.hauptantiek.com

www.hoofstockvet.com

www.vosflips.com

www.abrasiveresource.com

Help for choosing a charity:

www.charitynavigator.org

www. nccs.urban.org

Some of my favorite charities:

www.freedomalliance.org

www.woundedwarriorproject.org

www.honorflight.org

www.redcross.org

www.humanesociety.org

www.suicidepreventionlifeline.org

Check out my other book:

www.websites4smallbusiness.us